GOOD HOUSEKEEPING
FAMILY
MICROWAVE
COOKERY

GOOD HOUSEKEEPING
FAMILY
MICROWAVE
COOKERY

EBURY PRESS
LONDON

Published by Ebury Press
National Magazine House
72 Broadwick Street
London W1V 2BP

First impression 1985

ISBN 0 85223 480 5 (hardback)
ISBN 0 85223 481 3 (paperback)

Consultant Editor – Cassandra Kent

Edited by – Laurine Croasdale, Rosaline Fishel

Illustrations by Haywood and Martin

Designed by Peter Hardman

Photography by Martin Brigdale

Cookery by Susanna Tee, Janet Sruth

Front cover photograph: spinach stuffed Saddle of lamb with green beans,
new potatoes and carrots
Recipe on page 58

Computerset by MFK Typesetting Ltd, Saffron Walden, Essex

*Printed and bound in Great Britain by Hazell Watson and Viney Limited,
Member of the BPCC Group, Aylesbury, Bucks*

CONTENTS

INTRODUCTION

Because domestically microwave cooking is a fairly new development, and because it differs so radically from conventional cooking, it tends to be regarded with some alarm. In fact, microwaving is easy to understand and a microwave oven is a most useful addition to virtually every type of household, and particularly for families who have a busy life-style.

MICROWAVES EXPLAINED

A microwave is a type of short-wavelength radiation similar in nature to radio waves. Microwaves are different from x-rays and gamma rays because they don't build up in the body.

Microwaves are produced by a device known as a magnetron which is housed inside the oven. Metal surfaces reflect microwaves, but food absorbs them; when microwaves are absorbed into food, the molecules of the food start to vibrate billions of

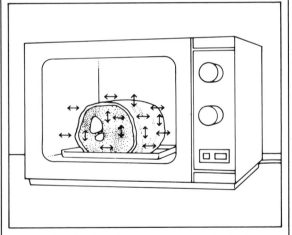

Food molecules vibrate, thus heating the food.

times a second. This makes the food heat up and cook, although the denser the food, the longer it takes to cook. Unlike conventional hobs and ovens, the microwaves enter the food on all its exposed surfaces. This is why it is important to arrange food in such a way that it gets the full benefit of the microwave energy (see page 10).

Why cook in a microwave oven?
Although the main advantage of cooking by microwave is speed, there are other advantages which make them a good choice for family cooking. These are:

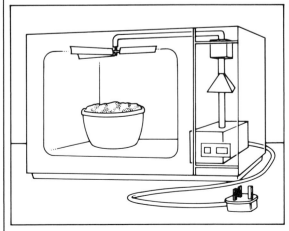

Microwaves are produced by a magnetron.

● They are cheap to run because they usually operate for only a few minutes at a time. So if you need to have hot food ready for members of the family who come in at different times, it is much cheaper to heat up each meal as it is required rather than to keep food warm in a conventional oven.

● They make the kitchen less hot than a conventional cooker and don't need to be used in the kitchen at all. You may find it more convenient to keep your microwave oven in the dining-room or family room.

● It is a very clean method of cooking. Many foods can be cooked in the dishes they are to be served in or eaten off thus cutting down on washing-up. And, because the heat goes straight into the food, it doesn't burn on to the cooking containers so they are always easy to clean. Providing you avoid letting fat spatter around the oven cavity when cooking for example joints and bacon, all you need do is wipe the oven out with a damp cloth from time to time.

● Cooking smells are reduced. This is particularly helpful in kitchens where there is little or no ventilation.

● Foods retain their nutrients, texture, shape, colour and flavour because they are neither subjected to lengthy cooking nor cooked in large quantities of water.

● Defrosting and reheating can be carried out in minutes. This makes it possible to prepare food quickly if you have unexpected guests.

● Microwave ovens are easy and safe to use. Children, elderly people and disabled people will find them particularly appropriate for this reason.

Microwave ovens are safe
It is because people don't understand how microwave ovens work that rumours have built up about their lack of safety. In fact, they are one of the safer kitchen appliances since they do not get hot, have no sharp edges to cut yourself on and switch off automatically when the door is opened.

You should choose a microwave oven which carries the BEAB (British Electro-technical Approvals Board) safety label which shows that the appliance has been built to comply with British Standard 3456 (BS 3456: Part 2: Section 2.33: 1976 'Microwave ovens'). This means that random samples of the model are regularly tested at the Electricity Council Appliance Testing Laboratories for both electrical safety and microwave leakage.

When a microwave oven is tested, the door is opened and closed 100,000 times and leakage is measured after every 10,000 operations. The interlocks on the door are tested in the same way. The way that microwave ovens are constructed means that if just one of the locks is faulty, the door will not close properly and the microwaves will not be activated.

Most manufacturers recommend that their microwave ovens are checked professionally once a year. Although it is possible to buy small devices with which the makers claim you can check your own microwave oven to ensure that any leakage is within the recommended level, this is not a good idea. These devices are easily damaged and, as a result, may give a false reading. Qualified service staff carry a special measuring device which is regularly checked and adjusted for accuracy. Some local council Environmental Health Departments also have this special equipment and you may be able to have your machine checked by them.

Note Some cardiac pace-makers are affected by microwave energy. These are mainly the early types that are no longer made. Nonetheless, if someone in the family has a pace-maker, they should check with their doctor whether it is likely to be affected.

TYPES OF OVEN

There are three types of microwave oven available at present. The most popular one is the countertop portable. Most of those sold are the microwave-only type but an increasing number now incorporate some kind of browning element and some ovens also have the facility to be switched to conventional cooking. Some models incorporate a shelf so that more food can be cooked at one time.

Which type you choose will depend on how complex you intend your microwave cookery to be and what back-up cooking facilities you have in terms of grill and oven. In general, most people buy a fairly simple microwave oven the first time round and graduate to a more comprehensive model second time round. The advantage of browning in a microwave is that it saves switching on a separate grill or oven to achieve a brown finish to dishes. It is cheaper to brown in a microwave than to use part of a conventional cooker.

The facility for switching between conventional cooking and microwave in the same oven gives you the chance to cook foods that you prefer cooked conventionally or which will not cook well in a microwave, but if you have a satisfactory separate cooker this facility is not really necessary. It is probably a good choice if you have a small kitchen and don't want a full-sized separate oven as well as a microwave.

Microwave ovens with shelves are more complicated to use than those without. Usually the food on the shelf gets more of the microwave energy than that on the base so you need to select foods which will cook together satisfactorily. Remember, timings will be different if cooking more than one item at a time. It is a good idea to put an item which needs cooking on the top shelf and one which simply needs reheating underneath. Do not place the foods directly above one another. An advantage of this kind of model is that the shelf can be removed and the oven used as a single cavity as well.

Some full-sized ovens have a microwave oven built in above the main conventional one and this can be helpful if you lack countertop space for a portable model. However, it may be difficult for short people to use it comfortably if they have to stretch up for stirring and turning.

A few conventional cookers have the facility to be switched over to microwave cooking and this development is expected to continue.

Features to look for

Different models have different features, some are important, others a matter of personal choice. Some appear complex initially but you will find them easy to use once you have mastered the various controls.

On/off control (power button): this switches the oven on and off. It may also start the cooling fan and activate the oven light but it does not usually start the cooking process. Not all appliances have this control.

Cook (start) control: this switches on the microwave energy for cooking but cannot be operated until the oven door is closed and the output and time controls have been set. If you open the oven door during the cooking period, you will need to reset the cook button.

Timer: this controls the cooking period and may be either the mechanical or digital type. You set the cooking time in minutes and/or seconds and when it is completed, a bell or buzzer sounds and sometimes a digital display flashes the word 'end'. If you choose a model with a mechanical timer it is important to check that it will operate for just a few

seconds; some of them will only do periods such as quarter and half minutes which can be too long for some processes.

Door: most countertop models have doors which open sideways, although some have drop-down or slide-up doors. Check which way the door opens and see that it is convenient for the position you want to put your oven in. All microwave ovens incorporate a safety mechanism which means that they cannot operate unless the door is completely shut.

Cooking space: the oven cavity size is important as you can't always tell how big it is by looking at the outside dimensions of the appliance. The oven is made of metal, sometimes with a plastic coating, and may have a removable floor, turn-table or shelf. Check that it will be easy to clean and, if you have a dishwasher, that the removable parts can be washed in it.

Light: all ovens have an interior light which comes on during the cooking process and allows you to see how the food is progressing. On some models the light comes on when you open the door, which is helpful for positioning food correctly and for checking whether it is done without having to remove it from the oven. On others, the light is only on while cooking is taking place.

Oven vent and filter: the vents are designed to allow moisture to escape from the oven during cooking. Vents may be positioned at the back, on the side, front or top of the oven and it is important that they are left clear so that they can work efficiently. Check where the vents are on the model you are thinking of buying and see that they are convenient for the position you want to put the microwave in. Vents on top mean you can't put the appliance under a wall cupboard, for example.

The filter (on some ovens only) allows cool air to pass into the oven cavity to maintain a low ambient temperature. It does not affect the temperature of the food which is cooking but keeps the components of the oven cool. The filter should be removed from time to time and cleaned. Follow the manufacturer's recommendations on this.

Power output: this is quoted in watts and is the amount of microwave energy which the magnetron produces. As a rough guide, you halve the *input* of watts quoted on the rating plate to produce the figure for the output. Most domestic microwave ovens have an output of about 600 watts and the recipes in this book have all been timed on microwave ovens of this wattage. (See the note at the front of the book.)

Turn-table: all microwave ovens have 'hot spots' and if food is left in just one position during cooking it will cook unevenly. If your oven does not have a turn-table or built-in stirrers or paddles

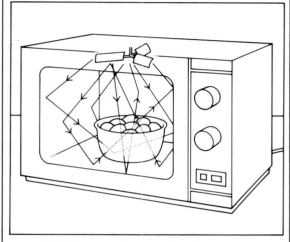

Built-in stirrers circulate the microwaves.

which move the microwaves around, you can buy a turn-table separately. Some models may not be used without their built-in turn-tables, others can, but in either case you need to turn the food by hand giving it a quarter turn three times during its cooking. This is especially the case with large items

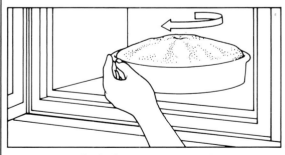

Turn the food to ensure even cooking.

of food such as flans, cakes, pâtés or large pieces of meat which cannot be stirred. It is useful to be able to remove the turn-table if you want to cook something which is too big to rotate, like a turkey, or something in an oval dish which will hit against the walls if put on a turn-table.

Browning dish: see page 16.

Temperature probe/food sensor: see pages 10 and 16.

Cooking guide: some microwave ovens have printed on their front a basic guide to the settings needed for cooking various common foods. This is only a guide since any cooking time depends on the weight and starting temperature of the food. But it can be helpful while you are getting used to this type of cooking or if the oven is likely to be used by a number of different people who may not be familiar with it.

Controls

The controls on a microwave oven may be dials, digital press-buttons or touch controls. The power settings are important. Very basic machines have just one setting so that you have to watch the food carefully, and when defrosting pulse the microwaves on and off so that they don't cook the food.

Some machines have a High and a Defrost setting but the most useful type of all have variable power settings which allow you to select the microwave energy output which best suits the food you are cooking. Unfortunately, the settings themselves have variable names, since manufacturers have not standardised them, but they tend to be terms like High, Reheat, Roast, Simmer, Bake, Defrost or High, Medium and Low. In this book the power settings used are HIGH, MEDIUM and LOW (see the note at the front of the book).

Memory controls are found on some machines. They are designed to allow you to cook food at two different power settings without having to alter them manually halfway through the cooking time.

Installing the oven

Follow the manufacturer's instructions for installation and take care to read the handbook thoroughly before attempting to use the appliance. Remember that microwave cooking is a much preciser function than cooking on a hob or in a conventional oven and that any do's or don't's should be followed.

Preparing food for microwave cooking

Most people who have cooked for years with a conventional hob and oven have forgotten that they had to learn how to prepare food for them. The same applies to preparing food for the microwave oven. Once you've got the hang of it, it becomes second nature and you don't have to think about it. The introductions to each chapter specify particular things that need doing to different types of food. On the following page are some golden rules which are the keynote to successful microwaving.

● Small, evenly shaped pieces of food will cook more successfully than large ones or those which are thick at one end and thin at the other. This is because the original strong microwave force penetrates the food only to a depth of 5 cm (2 inches); thereafter cooking is done by the molecules vibrating and producing heat, and in thick pieces of food they gradually become weaker

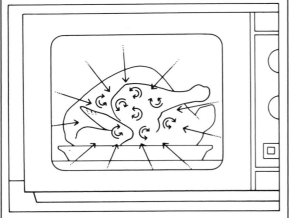

Vibrating molecules produce heat to cook food.

and consequently the food takes longer to cook. It is therefore important to arrange food for maximum exposure to the microwaves, with the thickest parts towards the sides of the oven cavity and the thinnest parts in the centre. Very thin parts may need to be protected with smooth pieces of foil to prevent them overcooking and drying out. Foil should never be allowed to touch the sides of the oven or it will distort the path of the microwaves and could damage the magnetron.

● Cooking times in a microwave oven depend on a number of factors which include the quantity of food, the density and the temperature at which it is put into the oven. The recipes in this book assume that ingredients are at room temperature, as appropriate, unless it is stated that they are frozen. When adapting recipes yourself bear in mind that a small quantity of food will cook more quickly than a large one. Do not assume that doubling the quantity means doubling the cooking time – some time is saved when larger amounts are cooked. In general, if a dish takes 10 minutes to cook and you double the quantity, allow 15 minutes. When cooking very large quantities there is often no saving in time compared with a conventional oven unless you are prepared to cook the food in a series of small batches. The larger the amount of food, the longer it will take to cook, and, because microwaves do not brown, it is not always possible

to tell when it is done. If your oven does not incorporate a temperature probe or sensor, it really is worth investing in a special microwave thermometer which can be used inside the oven (see page 16) or, alternatively, an ordinary meat thermometer which can be used outside the oven to check that the food is done. Food which has been refrigerated or which has just completed thawing will be considerably cooler than room-temperature ingredients and will take correspondingly longer to cook. It is important always to under- rather than to overcook food. Burnt offerings – and you may not spot them until they are cut open – cannot be retrieved, but undercooked food can be popped back in the oven for the few seconds or minutes necessary to achieve good results.

● Because microwave cooking is so quick, seasonings tend not to have enough time to become absorbed. Because of this it is better to under-season rather than to risk an overpowering flavour of condiments, herbs or spices. Another point, since water attracts salt and microwaves are affected by water, it is important to add salt at the end of the cooking time. Otherwise it may distort the pattern of the microwaves and lead to uneven cooking.

Microwave ovens and other kitchen equipment
In spite of what some manufacturers claim, for most people a microwave oven is not a replacement for a conventional cooker but a complement to it. Although you can cook a large number of dishes in the microwave, some dishes, such as soufflés and batter recipes like fritters and Yorkshire pudding, do not cook successfully and are best cooked on a hob or in a conventional oven. Using the microwave in conjunction with a conventional oven can often produce good results.

Microwaves and freezers
You can use the microwave in conjunction with the freezer in several ways: by using just the microwave to prepare the food for the freezer; by cooking conventionally, then freezing the food and reheating it in the microwave; by buying ready-frozen foods for cooking in the microwave and by using it for blanching fresh fruit and vegetables before freezing them.

When freezing food that you plan to microwave at a later date, it is useful to pack it in small portions, if possible. You can always microwave two or three individual portions together if required but it is much harder to cut off just the right amount needed for one person from a large, frozen piece. Not all of the plastic containers which are suitable for freezer storage can be used for cooking in the microwave. Neither should you use aluminium foil containers in it. Line these with either cling film or a polythene bag so that the contents can be lifted out. Or freeze food in the cooking dish itself, lined with cling film, so that the dish can be released for general use until required for that specific dish. The ideal container is one that can go directly from the freezer to the microwave to the table for serving and finally into the dishwasher. Because microwave heat is not in direct contact in the same way that a pan base is with its heat source, there is no burning on when cooking by microwave and suitable dishes wash easily and well in a machine.

For some dishes you may prefer to use a conventional cooker to prepare food which can be frozen and then reheated in the microwave. Traditional cakes and breads benefit from the crisping and browning that a conventional oven produces and bulk cooking of certain dishes like cakes, biscuits and bread will be as quick and no more trouble prepared conventionally.

A slow cooker is a useful adjunct to a microwave since it can be used, very cheaply, to produce dishes which require long, slow gentle cooking to tenderise meat and root vegetables and allow flavours to intermingle properly. Dishes like oxtail stew, carbonnade of beef and casserole of boiling fowl will have greater depth of flavour and better texture if cooked like this, frozen and then reheated by microwave when required.

Stock can be prepared in large quantities and cooked gently for hours in a large pan on a hob or in smaller quantities and less time in a pressure cooker. The rich, jellied stock produced can be frozen in quantities ranging from a few tablespoons for sauces to larger quantities for soups to be made at a later date in the microwave.

Barbecues can take hours, particularly if you are cooking thick chops or pieces of chicken. Start them off in the microwave and finish them on the barbecue grill to get the benefits of both quick, thorough cooking *and* the fine flavour of charcoal grilling.

Non-cooking appliances also work well in conjunction with a microwave. A blender or food processor can make soup in minutes. Soften the ingredients in the microwave, blend them to a purée and then return them to the microwave to cook them. Similarly, a food processor can be used to whip up a quick cake, pizza base, crumble topping or sponge pudding for immediate microwaving. Sauce ingredients can be whirled in a blender or processor, then cooked; onions and other vegetables can be chopped for a casserole or braise.

Special advantages of microwaves
A microwave oven is very economical. Not only does it cook for considerably shorter periods than a conventional oven, but it runs off a 13 or 15 amp socket outlet (as opposed to a 45 amp one) and uses less electricity, even for the same amount of time.

Time saving is, of course, the biggest plus for families which lead busy lives: food can be prepared quickly and easily and individual portions can be heated up or defrosted in a matter of minutes.

Another advantage is that everyone can cook their food. Because the inside of a microwave oven does not get as hot as a conventional oven, it's safe for children to use as long as they appreciate the need for oven gloves (necessary because the food conducts heat to its container).

Because it's so simple to use – just set the power setting and timer and switch it on – anyone can operate it. And, because the food can be ready-prepared – even set on the plates it's to be eaten from – there's virtually no mess and no clearing up.

Microwave ovens are particularly useful for disabled people. They can be put on a trolley at a suitable height, and the controls can be converted to braille on some models. Ask the oven manufacturer or the Royal National Institute for the Blind, 224 Great Portland Street, London W1N 6AA (01-388 1266) about this.

A microwave oven is also useful if someone in the family is on a special diet, be it a slimming one or a medical one such as low fat or low salt (especially good in a microwave as cooking is done without added salt). No longer does cooking something different for one member of the family become a major problem. Diet meals can either be prepared in advance and frozen for reheating or made from scratch in just a few minutes.

Another advantage is that faddy members of the family can be catered for more easily. If, for example, someone dislikes the chilli in chilli con carne you can, when making up a batch for freezing, reserve several portions without chilli and freeze them for separate reheating later.

From a nutritional point of view, a microwave is a real star. It cooks so quickly that there is little time for nutrients to be lost, and because foods such as vegetables are not broken down, they retain nutrients as well as shape and texture. Cooking liquids are kept to a minimum so few nutrients are lost when they are drained off. Vitamins that are water-soluble are less likely to disappear when microwaved, and vitamins that are heat sensitive stand a better chance of surviving than when subjected to lengthy cooking.

Oven cleaning is one of the most hated

household chores and microwaves score highly here. Most foods are covered during cooking and so do not dirty the oven. If something overflows, is spilled or spatters on to the inside of the oven, it will not burn on because the oven cavity itself does not get hot. Most spills can just be wiped up with a damp cloth, but any that prove obstinate can be removed by placing a bowl of water with a dash of lemon juice in the oven and microwaving on High until it boils. The steam produced will loosen any stains and the cavity can be wiped out with a cloth. Take care not to use a cloth with grit or sharp crumbs on it as this may scratch the oven lining which may in turn distort the path of the microwaves.

Standing time

Because of the way microwaves work, food continues to cook after the power has switched off – this is called 'standing time' – and it is essential to allow for this when calculating cooking time or food will overcook. Another purpose of standing time is to allow the heat inside the food to equalise itself. When a standing time of more than 2–3 minutes is specified, the food should be covered to allow this

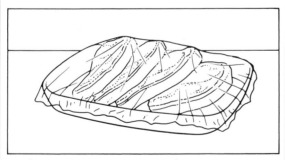

The food continues cooking during standing time.

to happen. When large joints and poultry are roasted, the heat inside will increase by about 5–7°C (10–15°F). For this reason do not worry if food removed from the oven looks uncooked. The standing time will correct this.

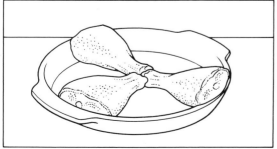

Arrange the food to expose the greatest area.

Arranging food

The way food is arranged in a microwave oven will dictate the speed at which it cooks. The greater the surface area that is exposed to the microwaves, the quicker it cooks. Ideally, food should be arranged in a ring or, if liquid, cooked in a ring mould so that microwaves can penetrate from the centre as well as from the outside surfaces. The thickest ends of foods such as chicken pieces and chops should be placed at the outside edge as they require longer cooking. Thinner edges may need protecting with

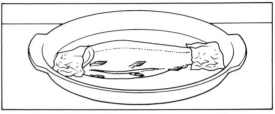

Cover thinner edges to prevent overcooking.

foil or else overlapping to prevent them cooking too quickly and drying out.

Cooking will be speeded up if food (which can be) is stirred at intervals to bring the bits in the

Stir food at intervals to speed up cooking.

middle which have absorbed less microwave energy to the outside. When cooking foods like meatballs or potatoes, reposition them halfway through the

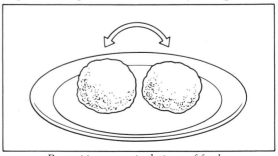

Re-position even-sized pieces of food.

cooking time so that those on the outside are on the inside and vice versa. Food should always be cooked in a single layer unless it is a liquid or in a mass, like vegetables. Most items should be turned over and items over 6 cm (2½ inches) thick should always be turned over halfway through the cooking time.

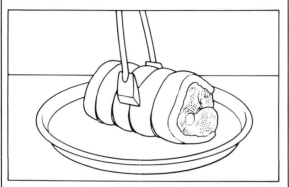

Turn thick pieces of food during cooking.

Cooking from frozen

One of the big advantages of a microwave oven is that it can defrost and reheat food in a matter of minutes so there's no need to think well in advance about getting food out of the freezer. Some items like frozen fish and vegetables can be cooked straight from frozen. Others, like poultry and joints of meat, need to be thawed before cooking. If you are cooking straight from frozen you will need to allow more cooking time than when cooking food that has already been thawed. Note, too, that when preparing food for the freezer, it is sensible to undercook it slightly to allow for further cooking to take place when reheating.

Some foods may need extra liquid added during the reheating time and you may want to make last-minute additions of ingredients such as mushrooms or cream.

You can cook in a surprising number of different materials in a microwave oven. The only ones which you can't use are those made of, or decorated with, metal since the microwaves cannot penetrate this and are reflected off it, back to the sides of the cabinet, where they could damage the magnetron. Whether you choose to buy special containers for microwave cooking or use those you already own will depend on what you have in your cupboards and what you want to cook. While many standard household materials are suitable for microwave cooking (see right), those materials which have been developed especially for microwaving will often transmit the waves more quickly and may be designed in special shapes which make cooking

Microwave equipment transmits waves quickly.

certain types of food easier. Another point, you are unlikely to own items like bun tins made of material other than metal.

Container shapes

The shape of the dishes in which you microwave food is important because of the way the microwaves bounce around the oven cabinet. Round containers are better than square ones since they have no corners in which microwaves can cluster and cause quicker cooking. Ring moulds are even better as they allow microwaves to reach the food through the inner ring as well as the outer. If you don't have a suitable container, you can create a similar effect by placing an upturned glass tumbler in the middle of a round container. Straight-sided containers cook food more evenly than those with sloping sides. With sloping sides the outer, shallower edge of the food will cook more quickly.

Shallow dishes cook food more quickly than deep ones as the food spreads out into a shallower level and offers a greater surface for the microwaves to penetrate. However, you can use this fact to regulate the cooking times of food, choosing a deeper container when you want something to cook more slowly.

Always use a dish that will be able to contain the food when it is hot and bubbling. The uncooked food should come no more than two-thirds of the way up the sides.

Glossary of materials

Durable microwave ware is designed as a long-lasting material and is frequently intended to be for freezer-to-oven-to-table use. It is made from various types of plastic and usually comes in a wide range of shapes and sizes specifically intended for microwaving different types of food. It is usually dishwasher-proof. The shapes most likely to be useful are listed under *Special shapes* (see page 16).

Semi-durable microwave ware is less robust than the durable type but is much cheaper and usually sold in bulk (fives, tens, etc). All types can be used in a freezer and some are dishwasher-proof. This type of ware is useful when you are cooking in bulk for the freezer but usually tends to be too pliable for use in dishes containing a lot of sugar or fat, both of which are affected by microwaves. It may also stain when used in conjunction with highly coloured ingredients like tomatoes or strawberries. The lack of rigidity also means this type of ware is not suitable for cooking liquids such as soup which make it distort.

Note Some of these types of special microwave ware are claimed to be suitable for use in a conventional oven or pressure cooker. Be sure to follow the manufacturer's instructions for this exactly and do not use in such a way unless it is specifically recommended.

Glass, especially ovenproof and ceramic glass, is very suitable for use in a microwave oven and with clear glass you can actually see how the food is cooking. Glass should only be used for short-term heating and never for foods containing fat or sugar as these reach high temperatures which will cause the glass to crack. Ovenproof types of glass can be stored in the freezer and taken straight from it to the microwave. Tough glass jugs can be used for measuring, mixing, cooking and even serving items such as gravy or custard. Never use glass with a metal trim or decoration in a microwave oven as it will cause arcing (sparks) and could damage the magnetron.

China and pottery are also suitable for microwave cooking although this may take longer than in, for example, durable microwave ware. Unglazed earthenware and pottery is usually porous and will absorb moisture from food (or washing-up) which will affect the microwaves on their passage through it and prevent them reaching the food. Carry out the water test (page 16) on any items you are not sure about.

Clay pots which need prior soaking in water are very successful for microwaving whole poultry or fish and for casseroles. Since clay absorbs moisture, and therefore microwaves, cooking is slowed down producing tender meat or fish. Soak the 'brick' according to the manufacturer's instructions before starting cooking. When calculating the cooking time, remember to make allowance for the fact that the clay will absorb some of the microwaves into its moisture and so more time will be needed for cooking. The brick itself will become hot because of this so be sure to use oven gloves when removing the lid to check progress. If you need to add extra liquid during the cooking period, make sure it is warmed first – cold liquid causes a rapid change in temperature which may crack the clay.

Plastics, unless specifically intended for microwave use, should be treated with care. In general, rigid plastics which will withstand boiling water and can be used in a dishwasher are suitable for microwave cooking, although brands such as *Melamine* and *Tupperware* are not. However, it is often possible to start gentle defrosting using a plastic which is not really suitable for microwaving and once the food is soft enough to be removed, it can be placed in another container.

Plastic baby bottles can be used to warm milk or juice but should not be sterilised in a microwave oven unless they particularly state that this is possible.

Polystyrene plates and cups can only be used for gentle warming of contents.

Plastic cooking pouches and bags are suitable for microwave use but should be pierced or slit first to let steam out and prevent pressure building up in case they burst. Do not use the metal tie tags supplied with them but fasten them with string or an elastic band which will not be affected by microwaves. Paper plates and cups may be used in the microwave for defrosting and gentle reheating but will not withstand prolonged heat and will burn. Take care with waxed and plasticised paper as the coating may melt in the oven. Disposable plastic cups are not suitable. Paper cake cases are best used double for small cakes.

Wood can be used in the microwave for short periods but the water in it will gradually evaporate and cause cracking. Regular light rubbing with salad oil should help keep it in good condition but it is best to limit its exposure to microwaves to just a few seconds now and again, for example when warming bread rolls. It is useful to be able to leave wooden spoons inside the oven in foods which need stirring at regular intervals. Wicker and straw can also be used in the microwave for short periods but will become brittle if left too long. Shells can be used for cooking small portions of fish dishes.

Cotton and linen napkins are fine for lining baskets when bread is to be warmed or when warm napkins are required. Do not leave them in too long and never expose fabrics containing synthetic fibres to microwaves as they may distort or melt.

Materials for covering food

Food should be covered in a microwave oven to retain its moisture and to prevent the top from drying out. The only items which do not need to be covered are bread and pastry which need to become dry during cooking. All the recipes in this book state whether the food should be covered or not and the recommendation should be followed for best results.

Non-metal lids may be used to cover food but should be put on at a slant if the recipe recommends that a vent should be left to allow steam to escape, and to leave a space for stirring. Take care when removing a lid that has been fitted tightly. There will be a blast of hot air, so tilt the lid away from you and protect hand and wrist with an oven glove.

Open the lid away from you.

Cling film makes a good lid in a microwave, with the added advantage that you can see the food

Carefully pull the cling film towards you.

through it. If the food is to be stirred, leave a corner folded back; otherwise, pierce a hole in it to allow steam to escape. If you do not do this, the cling film will stick to the food as soon as the cooking is finished and it can be quite difficult to remove. Another point, take care when removing it as the steam may scald your hands. Start on the side furthest away from you and pull back the cling film towards you.

Absorbent kitchen paper makes a good lid for dishes which don't need a tight cover to keep moisture in. It is particularly useful when cooking foods such as bacon and sausages as it prevents fat

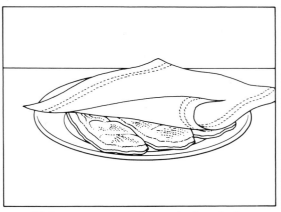

Kitchen paper is a good cover for fatty foods.

spattering all over the oven but doesn't trap air so that they don't become crisp. Remove it as soon as the food is cooked to prevent it sticking. It is also good for preventing bread, bread products, cakes and pastry from becoming soggy during reheating. Paper napkins can also be used, but avoid coloured ones as the moisture produced may cause the dye to run into the food or to stain the floor of the oven.

Aluminium foil, a great standby when cooking conventionally, needs to be used with care in a microwave. Small, smooth pieces can be used, shiny side in, to shield thin parts of food from cooking more quickly than the rest and to slow down cooking on certain things. It is vital that the foil does not touch the base, sides or roof of the oven cavity or it will affect the path of the microwaves and could damage the magnetron. Stop cooking immediately if arcing occurs because you have used too much foil.

Waxed or greaseproof paper can also be used for preventing food spattering. Do not expose waxed paper to prolonged cooking or the coating may melt into the food.

Special shapes

There are certain items which are not necessary for conventional cooking but which make microwave cooking easier. Not all are essential but as your microwave cookery skills develop you may find that some of them will help. A browning dish or skillet is made of glass ceramic with a special tin oxide coating on the underside which absorbs microwave

Use a browning dish for a golden finish.

energy when it is preheated without food in the oven – this takes up to 10 minutes. Without removing the dish from the oven, food is placed on it and it browns immediately – as it will under a preheated grill or on a barbecue. This is useful for foods such as chops, bacon, steaks and sausages which tend to look pallid even when cooked because the cooking time has been too short to allow them to brown. Take care when handling a browning dish which has been heated as it becomes very hot, and don't put it on to a kitchen surface that isn't heatproof. Don't scour it when cleaning – follow the manufacturer's instructions or rub it gently with a paste made of bicarbonate of soda and water and take care not to scratch the dish.

Roasting racks have a ridged surface which allows air to circulate around the food and prevents foods sitting in their own juices or fat. They are used when defrosting large, solid items such as a chicken or turkey and when roasting meat or poultry. You can buy special roasting dishes which have a tray to catch juices and will take a large joint or chicken, and small racks which need to be placed on a plate when cooking bacon or chops and are especially useful for putting inside roasting bags to prevent food sitting in its juices.

Plate rings are circles of plastic which enable you to cook plates of food one above the other.

A microwave thermometer is specially designed so that it will not be affected by microwaves.

Use plate rings to cook several plates of food.

Ordinary cooks' thermometers cannot be used in a microwave oven as the mercury is affected by the waves. With a microwave thermometer you can see through the door how cooking is progressing on a joint of meat or poultry and judge at what stage you need to remove it to allow it to complete cooking during standing time. You can, of course, use an ordinary meat thermometer to calculate this but only after you have removed the food from the oven. Some ovens have built-in temperature probes which cause the oven to switch off when the food reaches the pre-set temperature or reduce the power so that the food just keeps warm until required.

A separate turn-table may be needed if you buy a model which doesn't have one or which also lacks paddles or stirrers.

Testing containers

You can check if a container is suitable for microwave use by carrying out this simple test. Place the container in the oven and beside it put a glass of water. Microwave on High for 1–2 minutes. If the water is hot and the dish still cool, it is very suitable for microwave cooking. If the water is hot and the dish slightly warm, the dish is suitable for microwave cooking for fairly short periods but will take longer than the first type to cook food. If the water stays cool and the dish becomes hot, this means that the microwaves have been attracted to moisture contained in the dish and so they will never get beyond the outside to cook the food. There is also the danger that, if used, this type of dish will eventually break in the oven because it becomes too hot.

Chilled pea and mint soup – A pale, creamy green soup garnished with peas and mint.
Recipe on page 28.

HOW TO USE THE RECIPES IN THIS BOOK WITH YOUR OVEN

UNDERSTANDING POWER SETTINGS AND HEAT CONTROLS

When manufacturers refer to a 700-watt oven they are referring to the oven's *power output;* its *input,* which is indicated on the back of the oven, is double that figure.

The higher the wattage of an oven the faster the rate of cooking, thus food cooked at 700 watts on full power cooks in twice the time as food cooked at 350 watts. That said, the actual cooking performance of one 700-watt oven may vary from another with the same wattage because factors such as oven cavity size affect cooking performance.

Unlike conventional ovens, the various microwave ovens have yet to be standardised. A HIGH or full power setting on one oven may be 500 watts, while on another model HIGH or full power may be 700 watts. The vast majority of ovens sold today are either 600-, 650- or 700-watt ovens but there are many ovens still in use which have between 400 and 500 watts.

In this book
HIGH refers to full power output of 600 – 700 watts.

MEDIUM corresponds to 60 per cent of full power.

LOW is 35 per cent of full power.

If your oven power output is lower than 600 watts, then you must allow a longer cooking and defrosting time for all recipes and charts in this book.

Note: unless otherwise specified the following applies to all recipes

- *Follow either metric or imperial measures for the recipes in this book as they are not interchangeable.*
- *All spoon measures are level unless otherwise stated.*
- *Size 3 and 4 eggs should be used except where otherwise stated.*
- *Plain or self-raising flour can be used unless otherwise stated. Use white, brown or wholemeal flour but see individual chapters for use in pastry, bread and cake making.*
- *Use white or brown granulated sugar unless otherwise stated.*
- *Brown or white breadcrumbs can be used unless otherwise stated.*

Serve this **Ratatouille** of aubergines, peppers, courgettes and tomatoes with Garlic bread.
Recipes on pages 34 and 97.

BASIC RECIPES

MEAT GRAVY

cooking juices from the joint
beef stock
15 ml (1 level tbsp) cornflour
gravy browning (optional)
salt and pepper

1 Collect the meat cooking juices from the joint and pour them into a large ovenproof measuring jug. Remove any fat.

2 Make up to 450 ml (¾ pint) with beef stock. Microwave on HIGH for 3 minutes or until boiling.

3 Blend the cornflour with a little water and then stir it into the stock.

4 Microwave on HIGH for 3 minutes until the gravy thickens. Stir once during cooking. Add a few drops of gravy browning for a darker colour if wished. Season to taste with salt and pepper.

Makes 450 ml (¾ pint).

CHICKEN GRAVY

giblets from 1 chicken, thawed
15 ml (1 level tbsp) cornflour

1 Put the giblets in a large ovenproof bowl with 450 ml (¾ pint) water. If including the chicken livers, prick or halve them first so that they do not explode. Three-quarters cover with cling film and microwave on HIGH for 30 minutes. Strain.

2 Blend the cornflour with a little cold water. Mix it into the stock and make up to 450 ml (¾ pint) with juices from the cooked poultry.

3 Microwave on HIGH for 3 minutes or until the gravy thickens. Stir occasionally during cooking.

Makes 450 ml (¾ pint).

BASIC MEAT SAUCE

15 ml (1 tbsp) vegetable oil
1 large onion, skinned and finely chopped
1 garlic clove, skinned and crushed
100 g (4 oz) streaky bacon, rinded and chopped
450 g (1 lb) minced beef
397 g (14 oz) can tomatoes
100 g (4 oz) mushrooms, sliced
5 ml (1 tsp) Worcestershire sauce
30 ml (2 level tbsp) tomato purée
5 ml (1 level tsp) dried mixed herbs
pinch of nutmeg
salt and pepper

1 Heat the oil in a large ovenproof glass bowl on HIGH for 30–60 seconds.

2 Stir in the onion, garlic and bacon, cover and cook on HIGH for 5–7 minutes or until the onion is soft.

3 Break up the meat and stir in. Cover and cook on HIGH for 2–3 minutes or until the meat is no longer pink. Drain off any excess fat.

4 Add the tomatoes with their juice and roughly break up, then add the remaining ingredients to the meat mixture.

5 Cover and cook on HIGH for a further 15–20 minutes or until cooked, stirring after 10 minutes if there is no turn-table.

Serving Suggestions

1 Over cooked rice or pasta, sprinkled with Parmesan.

2 As a base for Shepherd's Pie – top with hot cooked mashed potato and brown under a preheated conventional grill.

3 As a sauce with pasta or rice – add 150 ml (¼ pint) red wine or stock at the end of step 3, bring to the boil and cook uncovered until thickened and reduced, stirring occasionally.

Serves 4.

ONE-STAGE WHITE SAUCE

Pouring sauce:
15 g (½ oz) butter or margarine
15 g (½ oz) plain flour
300 ml (½ pint) milk
salt and pepper

Coating sauce:
25 g (1 oz) butter or margarine
25 g (1 oz) plain flour
300 ml (½ pint) milk
salt and pepper

1 Put all the ingredients in an ovenproof measuring jug or small bowl and blend well together.

2 Microwave on HIGH for 3½–4½ minutes or until the sauce has boiled and thickened, stirring after every minute.

Variations
Add the following to the hot sauce with the seasoning:

Cheese sauce: 50 g (2 oz) grated mature Cheddar cheese and a pinch of mustard powder.

Parsley sauce: 30 ml (2 tbsp) chopped fresh parsley.

Hot tartare sauce: 15 ml (1 tbsp) chopped fresh parsley, 10 ml (2 tsp) chopped gherkins, 10 ml (2 tsp) chopped capers and 15 ml (1 tbsp) lemon juice.

Caper sauce: 15 ml (1 tbsp) capers and 5–10 ml (1–2 tsp) vinegar from the jar of capers.

Blue cheese sauce: 50 g (2 oz) crumbled Stilton or other blue cheese and 10 ml (2 tsp) lemon juice.

Mushroom sauce: 75 g (3 oz) sliced, lightly cooked mushrooms.

Onion sauce: 1 medium chopped cooked onion.

Egg sauce: 1 finely chopped hard-boiled egg.

Makes 300 ml (½ pint).

BREAD SAUCE

Serve hot with roast chicken, turkey and game dishes.

6 cloves
1 medium onion, skinned
4 black peppercorns
few blades of mace
450 ml (¾ pint) milk
25 g (1 oz) butter or margarine
100 g (4 oz) fresh breadcrumbs
salt and pepper
30 ml (2 tbsp) single cream (optional)

1 Stick the cloves into the onion and place it in a medium ovenproof glass bowl together with the peppercorns and mace. Pour in the milk. Microwave on HIGH for 5 minutes, stirring occasionally, until hot.

2 Remove the milk from the oven, cover and leave to infuse for at least 30 minutes.

3 Discard the peppercorns and mace and add the butter and breadcrumbs. Mix well, cover and microwave on HIGH for 3 minutes or until thickened, whisking after every minute. Remove the onion, season to taste and stir in the cream, if using. Leave to stand for 2 minutes.

Makes 450 ml (¾ pint).

HOLLANDAISE SAUCE

125 g (4 oz) butter
30 ml (2 tbsp) lemon juice or white wine vinegar
2 egg yolks
salt and pepper

1 Put the butter in an ovenproof glass bowl and microwave it on HIGH for 1–1½ minutes until it is melted.

2 Remove the butter from the oven and whisk in the lemon juice or wine vinegar and egg yolks.

3 Microwave on HIGH for 30–45 seconds or until the sauce is just thick enough to coat the back of a spoon. Stir briskly after each 15 seconds.

4 Season to taste before serving.

Serves 4.

SWEET WHITE SAUCE

20 g (¾ oz) butter or margarine
30 ml (2 level tbsp) plain flour
300 ml (½ pint) milk
25 ml (1½ level tbsp) sugar

1 Combine all the ingredients in an ovenproof measuring jug or glass bowl, blending well together.

2 Microwave on HIGH for 3½–4½ minutes or until the sauce has boiled and thickened, stirring after every minute.

Variations
Flavour with any of the following when the sauce has thickened:
5 ml (1 level tsp) mixed spice, ground nutmeg or ground cinnamon
30 ml (2 level tbsp) jam
grated rind of ½ an orange or lemon
30 ml (2 tbsp) single cream
15–30 ml (1–2 tbsp) rum

Makes 300 ml (½ pint).

CUSTARD SAUCE

15–30 ml (1–2 level tbsp) sugar
30 ml (2 level tbsp) or 600 ml (1 pint) packet custard
  powder
568 ml (1 pint) milk

1 Blend the sugar and custard powder, with a little of the measured milk, in an ovenproof measuring jug or glass bowl.

2 Stir in the rest of the milk.

3 Microwave the sauce on HIGH for 3–4 minutes or until thickened, stirring after every 2 minutes. Stir well and serve.

Makes 568 ml (1 pint).

CHOCOLATE SAUCE

15 ml (1 level tbsp) cornflour
15 ml (1 level tbsp) cocoa powder
30 ml (2 level tbsp) sugar
300 ml (½ pint) milk
knob of butter

1 In an ovenproof measuring jug or glass bowl blend the cornflour, cocoa and the sugar with enough of the milk to give a smooth paste.

2 Stir in the remaining milk and the butter.

3 Microwave on HIGH for 3–4 minutes or until the sauce is thickened, stirring every minute. Stir well and serve.

Makes 300 ml (½ pint).

JAM OR MARMALADE SAUCE

100 g (4 oz) jam or marmalade
2.5 ml (½ level tsp) arrowroot or cornflour
few drops of lemon juice

1 Place the jam or marmalade and 150 ml (¼ pint) water in an ovenproof glass bowl and microwave on HIGH for 2 minutes.

2 Blend the arrowroot or cornflour with 30 ml (2 tbsp) water until smooth and then stir it into the heated mixture.

3 Microwave on HIGH for 1–2 minutes or until boiling, stirring after 1 minute.

4 Add lemon juice to taste, and sieve if preferred before serving.

Serves 4.

SPICY TOMATO CHUTNEY

700 g (1½ lb) green tomatoes, skinned and roughly
  chopped
225 g (8 oz) cooking apples, peeled, cored and chopped
1 large onion, skinned and chopped
125 g (4 oz) soft dark brown sugar
125 g (4 oz) sultanas
50 g (2 oz) raisins
5 ml (1 level tsp) salt
200 ml (7 fl oz) malt vinegar
2 small pieces of dried root ginger
1.25 ml (¼ level tsp) cayenne pepper
2.5 ml (½ level tsp) mustard powder
2.5 ml (½ level tsp) chilli powder

1 Mix all the ingredients together in a large glass ovenproof bowl. Three-quarters cover with cling film and microwave on HIGH for 45 minutes or until the mixture is thick and all the liquid has been absorbed, stirring frequently.

2 Leave the chutney to stand, covered, for 15 minutes, then stir well and pot in the usual way.

Makes about 900 g (2 lb).

BASIC VICTORIA SANDWICH CAKE

175 g (6 oz) self-raising flour
175 g (6 oz) butter or margarine, softened
175 g (6 oz) caster sugar
3 eggs
30–45 ml (2–3 tbsp) milk
jam, to fill
icing sugar, for dusting

1 Grease a 19 cm (7½ inch) deep soufflé dish and line the base with greased greaseproof paper.

2 Mix together the flour, butter, sugar, eggs and 30 ml (2 tbsp) milk in a mixing bowl. Beat until smooth. If necessary, add an extra 15 ml (1 tbsp) milk to give a soft dropping consistency.

3 Spoon the mixture into the prepared dish and microwave on HIGH for 5½–7½ minutes or until a wooden cocktail stick inserted into the centre comes out clean. Give the dish a quarter turn every 2 minutes during cooking.

4 Leave to stand for 10 minutes, then turn out on to a wire rack, remove the paper and leave to cool.

5 When completely cold, split in half and fill with jam. Sieve icing sugar over the top of the cake.

Variations
Orange or lemon
Replace some of the milk with the juice and the grated rind of 1 orange or 1 lemon and proceed as above. When cold, split and fill with orange or lemon flavoured butter cream.

Chocolate
Replace 45 ml (3 level tbsp) of flour by 45 ml (3 level tbsp) of cocoa. Sandwich together with vanilla or chocolate butter cream. For a moister cake, blend the cocoa with water to give a thick paste. Beat into the creamed ingredients.

Coffee
Add 10 ml (2 level tsp) instant coffee dissolved in a little warm water to the creamed mixture with the egg. Or use 10 ml (2 tsp) coffee essence.

Serves 6–8.

BASIC SPONGE PUDDING

50 g (2 oz) soft tub margarine
50 g (2 oz) caster sugar
1 egg, beaten
few drops of vanilla flavouring
100 g (4 oz) self-raising flour
45–60 ml (3–4 tbsp) milk

1 Beat together the margarine, sugar, egg, vanilla flavouring and flour until smooth. Gradually add the milk to give a soft dropping consistency.

2 Spoon into a greased 600 ml (1 pint) pudding basin and level the surface.

3 Microwave on LOW for 7–9 minutes or until the top of the sponge mixture is only slightly moist and a wooden cocktail stick inserted in the centre comes out clean.

4 Leave to stand for 5 minutes before turning out on to a heated serving dish. Serve with Custard sauce (see page 21).

Serves 3–4.

Variations
Essex pudding
Spread jam over the sides and base of the greased pudding basin.

Apricot sponge pudding
Drain a 411 g (14½ oz) can of apricot halves and arrange them in the base of the greased pudding basin.

Syrup sponge pudding
Put 30 ml (2 tbsp) golden syrup into the bottom of the basin before adding the mixture. If you wish, flavour the mixture with the grated rind of a lemon.

Chocolate sponge pudding
Blend 60 ml (4 level tbsp) cocoa powder to a smooth cream with 15 ml (1 tbsp) hot water; add gradually to the creamed fat and sugar.

Jamaica pudding
Add 50–100 g (2–4 oz) chopped stem ginger with the flour.

Lemon or orange sponge
Add the grated rind of 1 orange or lemon when creaming the fat and sugar.

SOUPS

Virtually all homemade soups can be produced successfully in a microwave, although if you are making large quantities or a soup containing a lot of solid root vegetables, it is unlikely to be much quicker using a microwave than preparing it conventionally, and almost certainly slower than making it in a pressure cooker.

It is important when making soup in a microwave to use a large, round, deep container which can accommodate the expansion of liquid. Where a number of ingredients are used in the soup the flavours will mingle better if the soup is made in advance, allowed to cool and then reheated when required.

Most home-made soups freeze well and can easily be thawed and reheated in the microwave. Reheating is quicker in individual cups or bowls so it is a good idea to freeze soup in individual portions. A good tip is to place a freezer bag in each of the soup bowls, add the cold soup and then freeze it. Remove the bowls for everyday use and then when you want the soup all you need do is peel off the bag and place the soup in the bowl for reheating. Note that 150 ml (¼ pint) soup takes about 6 minutes on High to thaw. Stir it well during thawing and subsequent reheating to ensure that the heat is evenly distributed. Even in microwave ovens with turn-tables or stirrers you can get a mug of soup that is hot on one side and cold on the other if it hasn't been stirred during microwaving. Soups which have been thickened with egg or which contain cream, soured cream, seafood, pulses or mushrooms should be reheated on a Medium setting as the High one normally used will cause curdling or the breaking up of solid ingredients.

DEFROSTING SOUPS

Type	Approximate time on HIGH setting	Special instructions
Soups	5 minutes per 300 ml (½ pint) 8 minutes per 900 ml (1½ pints)	*Shake* and *stir* frequently during defrosting. *Add* cream or yogurt after defrosting.

MINESTRONE

2 small leeks, trimmed, washed and finely sliced
1 carrot, peeled and cut into 0.5 cm (¼ inch) dice
2 celery sticks, washed, trimmed and thinly sliced
3 streaky bacon rashers, rinded and chopped
25 g (1 oz) butter or margarine
1 garlic clove, skinned and crushed
2.5 ml (½ level tsp) dried basil
900 ml (1½ pints) boiling chicken stock
226 (8 oz) can tomatoes
213 g (7.5 oz) can red kidney beans, drained
salt and pepper
50 g (2 oz) long grain rice
50 g (2 oz) shelled fresh or frozen peas
30 ml (2 tbsp) chopped fresh parsley
25 g (1 oz) Parmesan cheese, grated

1 Put the leeks, carrot, celery and bacon into a large ovenproof glass bowl and add the butter, garlic and basil. Three-quarters cover with cling film and microwave on HIGH for 15 minutes or until the carrot begins to soften. Stir the ingredients two or three times during cooking.

2 Stir in the stock, the tomatoes with their juice and the beans and season with salt and pepper. Microwave on HIGH for 10 minutes or until the vegetables are soft, stirring once during cooking.

3 Add the rice, peas and parsley. Stir well and microwave on HIGH for 5 minutes or until the pasta is tender. Stir the soup once during cooking. Leave it to stand for 5 minutes, then serve sprinkled with the cheese.

Serves 6.

BORSCH (BEETROOT SOUP)

6 small raw beetroot, about 1 kg (2¼ lb), peeled
2 medium onions, skinned and chopped
1.1 litres (2 pints) beef stock
salt and pepper
30 ml (2 tbsp) lemon juice
90 ml (6 tbsp) dry sherry
150 ml (¼ pint) soured cream
snipped fresh chives, to garnish

1 Grate the beetroot directly into a 2.8 litre (5 pint) ovenproof glass bowl. Add the onions, stock, salt and pepper. Three-quarters cover the bowl with cling film and microwave on HIGH for 20–25 minutes until the beetroot and onions are very tender, stirring frequently.

2 Strain, discard the vegetables and add the lemon juice and sherry to the liquid. Adjust the seasoning. Serve either hot or chill in the refrigerator for at least 2 hours and serve cold. Serve garnished with a whirl of soured cream and a sprinkling of snipped chives.

Serves 4.

CREAM OF CELERY SOUP

25 g (1 oz) butter or margarine
1 large head celery, washed, trimmed and thinly sliced
1 medium onion, skinned and chopped
900 ml (1½ pints) chicken stock
300 ml (½ pint) milk
salt and pepper
bouquet garni
60 ml (4 tbsp) single cream
celery leaves or parsley, to garnish

1 Put the butter into a 2.8 litre (5 pint) ovenproof glass bowl and microwave on HIGH for 45 seconds until the butter melts. Add the celery and onion and stir well to coat evenly with the butter. Cover with cling film, pulling back one corner to vent. Microwave on HIGH for 6–8 minutes until the celery softens, stirring frequently.

2 Add the chicken stock, milk, salt, pepper and bouquet garni to the celery. Three-quarters cover the bowl with cling film and microwave on HIGH for 18–20 minutes until the celery is very soft.

3 Cool the soup slightly, remove the bouquet garni and then purée in a blender or food processor, or rub through a sieve.

4 Return the soup to a clean, ovenproof serving bowl and reheat on HIGH for 2 minutes.

5 Stir the cream into the soup. Serve garnished with chopped celery leaves or parsley.

Serves 4.

CAULIFLOWER SOUP

50 g (2 oz) butter or margarine
1 medium onion, skinned and finely chopped
30 ml (2 level tbsp) flour
750 ml (1¼ pints) chicken stock
1 small cauliflower, broken into florets
salt and pepper
30 ml (2 tbsp) single cream
chopped fresh parsley, to garnish

1 Place the butter in a large ovenproof glass bowl and microwave on HIGH for 45 seconds until melted. Stir in the onion, cover with cling film, pulling back one corner to vent, and microwave on HIGH for 5–7 minutes until softened.

2 Stir in the flour and microwave on HIGH for 1 minute. Gradually stir in the stock and microwave on HIGH for 3–4 minutes, stirring occasionally, until boiling and thickened.

3 Place the cauliflower in an ovenproof glass bowl, cover with cling film, pulling back one corner to vent, and microwave on HIGH for 7–8 minutes, stirring occasionally, until softened.

4 Add the cauliflower to the sauce and microwave on HIGH for 4 minutes. Allow the soup to cool for about 5 minutes, then pour it into a food processor or blender and purée until smooth. Season well with salt and pepper.

5 Return the soup to a clean ovenproof glass bowl. Microwave on HIGH for 2–3 minutes to reheat the soup. Stir in the cream. Serve garnished with parsley.

Serves 4–6.

WATERCRESS AND ORANGE SOUP

50 g (2 oz) butter or margarine
1 large onion, skinned and chopped
2 large bunches of watercress, trimmed, washed and
  chopped
45 ml (3 level tbsp) flour
salt and pepper
1.1 litres (2 pints) chicken stock
grated rind and juice of 1 medium orange
3 slices white bread
150 ml (¼ pint) single cream

1 Put the butter into a 2.8 litre (5 pint) ovenproof glass bowl and microwave on HIGH for 45 seconds until the butter melts. Add the onions, cover with cling film, pulling back one corner to vent, and microwave on HIGH for 5–6 minutes until the onions soften.

2 Add the watercress to the onions, cover and microwave on HIGH for 1–2 minutes. Stir in the flour, salt, pepper and stock. Three-quarters cover with cling film and microwave on HIGH for 8 minutes, stirring frequently.

3 Add the orange rind and 45 ml (3 tbsp) orange juice to the soup. Allow to cool for about 5 minutes, then purée in a blender or food processor until smooth.

4 Cut the bread into small cubes and grill until golden.

5 Return the soup to a clean ovenproof glass bowl and stir in the cream. Microwave on LOW for 6–7 minutes, stirring frequently, until hot but not boiling.

6 Serve the soup either hot or well chilled, garnished with the toasted croûtons.

Serves 6.

GERMAN LENTIL SOUP

3 rashers streaky bacon, rinded and diced
1 large onion, skinned and sliced
1 large carrot, peeled and sliced
3 celery sticks, washed, trimmed and sliced
350 g (12 oz) lentils, washed
2.5 ml (½ level tsp) dried thyme
2 bay leaves
1.4 litres (2½ pints) chicken stock
15 ml (1 tbsp) lemon juice
salt and pepper

1 Put the bacon, onion, carrot and celery into a 2.8 litre (5 pint) ovenproof glass bowl and mix together well. Cover with cling film, pulling back one corner to vent. Microwave on HIGH for 8 minutes until the vegetables soften, stirring once or twice.

2 Add the lentils, herbs and chicken stock to the vegetables. Three-quarters cover with cling film and microwave on HIGH for about 10 minutes until boiling, stirring well. Reduce the setting and microwave on LOW for 40–50 minutes until the lentils are very soft. Remove and discard the bay leaves.

3 Stir in the lemon juice. Season to taste with salt and pepper and serve.

Serves 4–6.

CORN CHOWDER

50 g (2 oz) butter or margarine
2 medium onions, skinned and sliced
100 g (4 oz) streaky bacon, rinded and diced
45 ml (3 level tbsp) flour
1.1 litres (2 pints) chicken stock
225 g (8 oz) potatoes, peeled and cut into 1 cm
  (½ inch) dice
175 g (6 oz) carrots, peeled and coarsely grated
335 g (11.8 oz) can sweetcorn, drained
150 ml (¼ pint) single cream
salt and pepper
chopped fresh parsley, to garnish

1 Put the butter into a 2.8 litre (5 pint) ovenproof glass bowl and microwave on HIGH for 45 seconds until the butter melts. Add the onions and the bacon. Cover with cling film, pulling back one corner to vent, and microwave on HIGH for 5–6 minutes until the onions are softened.

2 Stir in the flour and microwave on HIGH for 1 minute, then gradually stir in the stock, potatoes and carrots. Three-quarters cover with cling film and microwave on HIGH for about 8 minutes until boiling, stirring frequently. Microwave on HIGH for a further 10–12 minutes until the potatoes are tender.

3 Add the sweetcorn and stir in the cream. Microwave on LOW for 3–4 minutes until heated through but do not boil.

4 Season the soup to taste with salt and pepper. Serve garnished with chopped parsley.

Serves 4–6.

LEEK AND POTATO SOUP

450 g (1 lb) leeks, trimmed, washed and thinly sliced
225 g (8 oz) potatoes, peeled and diced
750 ml (1¼ pint) milk
150 ml (¼ pint) chicken stock
salt and pepper

1 Place the leeks and potatoes in a large ovenproof glass bowl. Cover them with cling film, pulling back one corner to vent, and microwave on HIGH for 10 minutes.

2 Add the milk and chicken stock and microwave on HIGH for 5–7 minutes until very hot. Allow the ingredients to cool for about 5 minutes, then pour them into a food processor or blender and purée until smooth. Season well with salt and pepper, then reheat the soup on HIGH for 2–3 minutes.

Serves 4–6.

LEMON SOUP

25 g (1 oz) butter or margarine
1 medium onion, skinned and thinly sliced
1 large carrot, peeled and thinly sliced
2 celery sticks, washed, trimmed and thinly sliced
2 lemons
1.1 litres (2 pints) chicken stock
2 bay leaves
salt and pepper
snipped chives and lemon slices, to garnish

1 Put the butter into a 2.8 litre (5 pint) ovenproof glass bowl. Microwave on HIGH for 45 seconds until the butter melts. Add the onions, carrot and celery and mix well. Cover with cling film, pulling back one corner to vent, and microwave on HIGH for 8 minutes until the vegetables soften.

2 Meanwhile, thinly pare the lemons using a potato peeler. Put the rinds in a small ovenproof bowl and pour over 300 ml (½ pint) boiling water. Cover and microwave on HIGH for 1½ minutes. Drain. Squeeze the juice from the lemons to give 75–90 ml (5–6 tbsp).

3 Add the blanched lemon rind and the juice, stock and bay leaves to the softened vegetables; season well. Three-quarters cover with cling film. Microwave on HIGH for about 8 minutes until boiling. Stir and microwave on HIGH for a further 10 minutes until the vegetables are very soft.

4 Cool the soup a little, remove the bay leaves and then purée in a blender or food processor until quite smooth.

5 Return the soup to a clean ovenproof glass bowl and stir in the cream. Microwave on LOW for about 5–6 minutes until hot but not boiling, stirring frequently. Adjust the seasoning to taste. Serve the soup hot or chilled, garnished with snipped chives and lemon slices.

Serves 4–6.

VEGETABLE SOUP

50 g (2 oz) butter or margarine
225 g (8 oz) carrots, peeled and finely diced
175 g (6 oz) swede, peeled and finely diced
2 small leeks, trimmed, washed and finely sliced
25 g (1 oz) flour
450 ml (¾ pint) chicken stock
300 ml (½ pint) milk
salt and pepper .
chopped fresh parsley, to garnish

1 Put the butter into a 1.7 litre (3 pint) ovenproof glass bowl and microwave on HIGH for 45 seconds until the butter melts.

2 Add the vegetables and lightly mix together. Three-quarters cover with cling film and microwave on HIGH for 8–10 minutes until the vegetables begin to soften, stirring two or three times.

3 Stir in the flour and stock. Microwave on HIGH for 10–15 minutes until the vegetables are very soft. Stir in the milk and season well with salt and pepper. Microwave on HIGH for 2–3 minutes until hot but not boiling. Serve sprinkled with chopped parsley.

Serves 4.

VICHYSSOISE

25 g (1 oz) butter or margarine
2 medium leeks, white parts only finely sliced and
   washed
1 small onion, skinned and finely chopped
350 g (12 oz) potatoes, peeled and finely sliced
600 ml (1 pint) chicken stock
salt and pepper
1 blade of mace
300 ml (½ pint) double cream
30 ml (2 tbsp) snipped fresh chives or finely chopped
   watercress, to garnish

1 Put the butter into a 1.7 litre (3 pint) ovenproof
glass bowl and microwave on HIGH for 45 seconds
until the butter melts.

2 Add the leeks and onion and mix together.
Cover with cling film, pulling back one corner to
vent, and microwave on HIGH for 5–7 minutes
until the leeks and onion are softened.

3 Add the potatoes, stock, salt, pepper and mace
and stir well. Three-quarters cover with cling film
and microwave on HIGH for 15–17 minutes until
the vegetables are very soft, stirring frequently.

4 Allow the soup to cool a little. Remove the blade
of mace, then rub through a fine sieve, or purée in
a blender or food processor. Pour the soup into a
clean bowl, cover and refrigerate for 3–4 hours, or
overnight, until well chilled.

5 Just before serving, stir in the cream. Serve
sprinkled with chives or watercress.

Serves 4.

CHILLED PEA AND MINT SOUP

50 g (2 oz) butter or margarine
1 medium onion, skinned and roughly chopped
450 g (1 lb) peas
568 ml (1 pint) milk
600 ml (1 pint) chicken stock
2 large fresh mint sprigs
pinch of caster sugar
salt and pepper
150 ml (¼ pint) natural yogurt
mint sprigs, to garnish

1 Put the butter into a 2.8 litre (5 pint) ovenproof
glass bowl and microwave on HIGH for 45 seconds
until the butter melts.

2 Add the onion and cover the bowl with cling
film, pulling back one corner to vent, and
microwave on HIGH for 5–7 minutes, or until the
onion is soft.

3 Add the peas, milk, stock, 2 mint sprigs and
sugar. Three-quarters cover with cling film and
microwave on HIGH for about 8 minutes until
boiling. Reduce the setting and microwave on
LOW for 15 minutes, until the peas are really
tender. Season well with salt and pepper and cool
slightly.

4 Remove about 45 ml (3 level tbsp) peas from the
soup and put them aside for the garnish. Rub the
remaining peas through a sieve, or purée them in a
blender or food processor until quite smooth.

5 Pour the purée into a large serving bowl. Adjust
the seasoning and leave to cool for 30 minutes. Stir
in the yogurt and cover and chill for 2–3 hours
before serving.

6 Serve garnished with the reserved peas and mint
sprigs.

Serves 4–6.

CHILLED CUCUMBER AND MUSHROOM SOUP

15 ml (1 tbsp) vegetable oil
1 small onion, skinned and finely chopped
1 garlic clove, skinned and crushed
1 cucumber, peeled and finely chopped
750 ml (1¼ pints) vegetable or chicken stock
salt and pepper
75 g (3 oz) mushrooms, chopped
150 ml (¼ pint) single cream
15 ml (1 tbsp) chopped fresh mint
few drops of green food colouring (optional)
mushroom slices, to garnish

1 Place the oil, onion and garlic in a large ovenproof bowl, three-quarters cover with cling film and microwave on HIGH for 5–7 minutes or until softened.

2 Add the cucumber and microwave on HIGH for 5 minutes or until the cucumber is slightly softened.

3 Stir in the stock and season well with salt and pepper. Three-quarters cover with cling film and microwave on HIGH for 6–7 minutes or until the cucumber is tender.

4 Leave for 5–10 minutes to cool slightly, then stir in the mushrooms. Purée the soup in a blender or food processor until smooth, then leave for 1–2 hours until cool.

5 Stir in the cream, mint, and food colouring, if using, adjust the seasoning and chill.

6 Ladle the soup into individual chilled bowls and serve garnished with mushroom slices.

Serves 4–6.

MELBA TOAST

4 thin slices of white bread

1 Toast the bread on both sides until golden brown.

2 Using a sharp knife, remove the crusts and slice the bread in half horizontally.

3 Place untoasted side up on a microwave baking sheet or a large ovenproof plate and microwave on HIGH for 30–40 seconds until dry and crisp.

Note: Melba toast may be made in advance and stored in an airtight container.

Serves 4.

To warm bread rolls, place them in a wicker basket ready for serving and microwave them on HIGH. Two rolls take 15–30 seconds, four rolls take 30–45 seconds and six rolls take 45 seconds–1½ minutes. Do not overheat the rolls or they will be dry.

GARLIC CROUTONS

25 g (1 oz) butter or margarine
1 small garlic clove, skinned and crushed
salt and pepper
2 thick slices of bread, crusts removed
paprika

1 Place the butter in a small ovenproof bowl and microwave on LOW for 15–20 seconds or until softened.

2 Beat in the garlic and season well with salt and pepper.

3 Butter the bread on both sides with the garlic butter. Cut each slice of bread into 12–16 squares depending on the size of the slice.

4 Spread the bread out on a sheet of greaseproof paper placed on a large flat ovenproof plate – you may need to cook half at a time if your oven is small.

5 Sprinkle the bread with paprika and microwave on HIGH for 1½–2 minutes until the croûtons are firm but not crisp. Re-position during cooking. Leave the bread to stand for 5 minutes. Top individual bowls of soup with 3–4 croûtons.

Serves 6–8.

STARTERS AND SNACKS

Convention usually suggests serving a cold starter at a dinner party where the other courses are hot, usually in order to leave the hosts free to join their guests for pre-dinner drinks. With a microwave oven, however, a hot starter becomes an attractive possibility. It could be either something which is cooked in advance and then reheated for a few minutes just before serving or a dish such as Corn-on-the-cob (see page 32) which takes less than 10 minutes to cook and can be served as a first course.

Snacks, too, are easily prepared in a microwave and are particularly good for filling up hungry children between meals. They are also excellent for making a quick supper dish, perhaps before rushing out to an evening class or when coming in hungry after the theatre.

Another point, there are innumerable starters and snacks which can be cooked in the microwave well in advance of when needed and then left to chill.

Eggs and cheese often form the basis of both types of dish. However, they are ingredients which need careful attention in the microwave: cooking them too hot or for too long can spoil them.

Eggs should never be cooked in their shells as microwaving causes pressure to build up so that they explode. When yolk and white are beaten together, as in scrambled eggs, a High setting can be used, but where yolk and white remain separate, a Medium to Low setting should be used. Before cooking the yolk, pierce it once or twice with the tip of a cocktail stick or sharp knife so that pressure does not build up inside the yolk membrane. This is necessary because unlike conventional cooking where the white cooks before the yolk, in microwaving the yolk cooks before the white. The reason for this is that the microwaves are attracted to the fat content in the yolk.

Eggs should always be cooked from room temperature. If they have been refrigerated, microwave them on High for 3 seconds – no more or they will explode – before cooking them. To slow up the cooking of eggs, place a glass of water in the microwave with them.

Cooking times for egg dishes should be followed scrupulously and allowance made if using a smaller or larger egg than specified in the recipe. Bear in mind that eggs continue to cook after the microwaves have stopped and that a difference of a few seconds can be critical in terms of spoiling a dish. It is always better to under- rather than overcook a dish.

Cheese also cooks in only a few seconds and since in most recipes it is merely required to melt, it can often be added towards the end of the cooking time. A more even cooking result is achieved if you grate rather than slice or dice cheese before adding it to a dish. Processed cheese, which has already been subjected to heat treatment, cooks more quickly than unprocessed. Where cheese is used as a topping it can be melted on the High setting, otherwise cook it on Low.

AUBERGINE DIP

900 g (2 lb) aubergines
salt and pepper
3 garlic cloves, skinned and crushed
60 ml (4 tbsp) olive oil
juice of ½ a lemon
chopped fresh parsley or 1 anchovy fillet, to garnish
celery, carrot and pepper sticks, to serve

1 Peel and dice the aubergines and place them in a colander or sieve. Sprinkle with salt and leave them to stand for 30 minutes, then rinse and drain them well on absorbent kitchen paper. Place the aubergines in a large mixing bowl and add 60 ml (4 tbsp) water and 1.25 ml (¼ level tsp) salt. Three-quarters cover with cling film and microwave on HIGH for 12–15 minutes until the aubergines are soft, stirring two or three times during the cooking time. Drain the aubergines and leave them to cool slightly.

2 Place the cooked aubergines in a blender, food processor or mortar, with the garlic. Blend them together, then slowly add the oil, drop by drop. Add the lemon juice and season with salt and pepper.

3 Turn the aubergine dip into a small serving bowl and chill before serving. Garnish with parsley or a rolled anchovy fillet. Place the bowl in the centre of a large plate and surround it with raw vegetables (crudités) neatly trimmed, for dipping.

Serves 6 as a starter.

CREAMY BACON DIP

225 g (8 oz) lean streaky bacon, rinded
225 g (8 oz) low fat soft cheese
150 ml (¼ pint) soured cream
2 gherkins, chopped
salt and pepper
15–30 ml (1–2 tbsp) mayonnaise
chopped fresh parsley, to garnish
potato crisps or celery, carrot and pepper sticks, to serve

1 Line a large ovenproof plate with several sheets of absorbent kitchen paper, lay the bacon rashers in a single layer on the paper and cover them with another layer of paper. Microwave on HIGH for 5–6 minutes until the bacon is cooked. Remove the bacon from the oven, quickly remove the paper and allow the bacon to cool.

2 Finely chop the bacon. Put the cheese in an ovenproof glass bowl and microwave on HIGH for 30 seconds – 1 minute until it is soft. Mix in the soured cream, gherkins and bacon. Season well with salt and pepper, and finally fold in the mayonnaise.

3 Spoon the dip into a serving bowl and garnish it with the parsley. Stand the bowl in the centre of a large plate and surround the bowl with crisps or the vegetable sticks for dipping.

Serves 6–8.

CHICKEN LIVER PATE

225 g (8 oz) chicken livers
125 g (4 oz) streaky bacon, rinded
1 medium onion, skinned and thinly sliced
15 ml (1 level tbsp) wholegrain mustard
15 ml (1 tbsp) brandy or sherry
1 garlic clove, skinned and crushed
salt and pepper
125 g (4 oz) butter or soft tub margarine
lemon slices and parsley sprigs, to garnish

1 Cut the liver and bacon into small pieces.

2 Place the liver, bacon and onion in a 1.7 litre (3 pint) microwave dish with the mustard, brandy or sherry, garlic and seasonings.

3 Cover and microwave on HIGH for 4 minutes and stir well. Re-cover and microwave on HIGH for a further 4 minutes until tender. Leave to cool.

4 Purée the mixture in a blender or food processor with the butter until smooth. Adjust seasoning.

5 Spoon into a serving dish, cover and chill in the refrigerator before serving. Garnish with lemon slices and parsley.

Serves 6.

HADDOCK PATE

225 g (8 oz) smoked haddock fillet
25 ml (5 tsp) lemon juice
225 g (8 oz) full fat soft cheese
15 ml (1 tbsp) chopped fresh parsley
salt and pepper

1 Place the haddock fillet in a buttered shallow ovenproof dish and sprinkle with 10 ml (2 tsp) of the lemon juice. Cover the top of the dish with cling film, pulling back one corner to vent. Microwave the fish on HIGH for 4–5 minutes until the haddock is cooked and the flesh flakes easily.

2 Drain the haddock well. Remove any skin, membrane and bones. Allow the fish to cool, then flake it finely.

3 Beat the cheese in a small mixing bowl until it is soft and creamy. Beat in the remaining lemon juice, the parsley and the flaked haddock. Season the mixture well with salt and pepper.

Serves 4–6.

CORN-ON-THE-COB WITH HERB BUTTER

4 corn on the cob
100 g (4 oz) butter, softened
salt and pepper
5 ml (1 tsp) lemon juice
45 ml (3 tbsp) finely chopped fresh mixed herbs – mint,
  parsley, lemon thyme and marjoram

1 Peel back the husks from the corn and remove the silk.

2 Beat the butter with the remaining ingredients. Spread the herb butter all over the ears of corn, then re-cover them with the green husks. If the cobs are without husks, wrap each one in greaseproof paper.

3 Place the corn cobs side by side in a shallow ovenproof dish and microwave on HIGH for about 8–9 minutes until the corn is tender, turning and re-positioning the cobs two or three times during the cooking time.

4 Remove the greaseproof paper, if used, or gently pull back the husks before serving.

Serves 4 as a starter or snack.

BROCCOLI AND EGGS

225 g (8 oz) broccoli
50 g (2 oz) butter or margarine
6 eggs, size 2
75 ml (5 tbsp) milk
salt and pepper
4 slices of hot toast, crusts removed

1 Trim the broccoli and cut it into neat, even-sized sprigs. Carefully peel off the tough outer skin from the stalks, peeling right up to the flower heads.

2 Place the broccoli sprigs in a shallow ovenproof dish and add 60 ml (4 tbsp) water. Cover the top with cling film, pulling back one corner to vent. Microwave the broccoli on HIGH for 4–5 minutes until the sprigs are just tender, rearranging them halfway through cooking.

3 Remove the cooked broccoli from the oven and keep it hot while cooking the eggs.

4 Put the butter into a medium ovenproof glass bowl and microwave on HIGH for 45 seconds until the butter melts. Add the eggs, milk, salt and pepper and lightly beat the ingredients together. Microwave them on HIGH for 3–4 minutes, stirring every 30 seconds and drawing the edges to the middle, until the eggs are only just set and are quite moist. Leave them to stand for 1–2 minutes. The eggs for this dish need to be very soft and creamy – if they are overcooked and dry, the dish will be spoilt.

5 Place the slices of toast on to individual serving plates. Reheat the broccoli on HIGH for ½–1 minute.

Marinated chicken with peanut sauce – These cubes of chicken are threaded onto bamboo skewers and served on a bed of lettuce garnished with lemon. Serve the sauce separately in a bowl. *Recipes on pages 40 and 110.*

Overleaf: **Seafood scallops** – Mushrooms and haddock, combined in a creamy white sauce, is served in individual gratin dishes and decorated with a border of piped potato. *Recipe on page 35.*

6 Divide the scrambled eggs evenly among the toast, spooning it on neatly. Garnish the eggs with the hot sprigs of broccoli and serve immediately.

Serves 4 as a snack.

FENNEL A LA GRECQUE

2 large heads of Florence fennel
45 ml (3 tbsp) vegetable oil
1 large onion, skinned and chopped
150 ml (¼ pint) red wine
30 ml (2 level tbsp) tomato purée
30 ml (2 tbsp) lemon juice
1 bay leaf
2.5 ml (½ tsp) chopped fresh basil
5 ml (1 level tsp) sugar

1 Trim the root and stalk ends off the fennel and reserve the leaves for garnish. Quarter the bulb and cut it into thin slices.

2 Put the oil and onion into a large casserole and cover with cling film, pulling back one corner to vent. Microwave on HIGH for 7 minutes until soft.

3 Add the sliced fennel and all the remaining ingredients except the fennel leaves to the onion and stir well. Three-quarters cover the top of the dish with cling film and microwave on HIGH for 6–8 minutes until boiling, then stir. Reduce the setting to LOW and Microwave for 12–14 minutes, stirring occasionally, until the fennel is just tender.

4 Garnish with the reserved fennel leaves and serve warm with French bread.

Serves 4 as a starter.

Overleaf: **Chicken fricassee** – Roast chicken pieces are served in a sauce with coriander, chick-peas and carrots. Garnish with coriander.
Recipe on page 40.

Okra with coconut – Whole okra is steamed with onions, grated coconut and coriander, for a quick and tasty side dish.
Recipe on page 83.

HAM AND LEEKS AU GRATIN

8 medium leeks, trimmed and washed
salt and pepper
8 slices of cooked ham
50 g (2 oz) butter or margarine
50 g (2 oz) flour
300 ml (½ pint) milk
nutmeg
100 g (4 oz) Gruyère or Cheddar cheese, grated
25 g (1 oz) fresh breadcrumbs
chopped fresh parsley, to garnish

1 Put the leeks in a shallow ovenproof dish, add 150 ml (¼ pint) water and season with a little salt and pepper. Cover the dish with cling film, pulling back one corner to vent, and microwave on HIGH for about 10–12 minutes until the leeks are very soft, turning them over and re-positioning them two or three times during the cooking time.

2 Drain the liquid from the leeks into a measuring jug and make up the amount to 300 ml (½ pint) with stock or water, if necessary. Leave the leeks to cool slightly.

3 When cool enough to handle, wrap each leek in a slice of ham and arrange them neatly in a shallow ovenproof dish.

4 Put the butter into a 1.1 litre (2 pint) ovenproof glass bowl, and microwave it on HIGH for 45 seconds until it has melted. Stir in the flour and microwave on HIGH for 45 seconds. Gradually whisk in the milk and the reserved cooking liquid. Microwave on HIGH for 1 minute, then whisk the mixture thoroughly. Continue to microwave on HIGH for about 5 minutes, whisking every 30 seconds until the sauce thickens.

5 Stir half of the cheese into the sauce and then season it with salt, pepper and a little grated nutmeg. Stir the sauce until the cheese melts.

6 Pour the sauce over the leeks and ham and sprinkle it with the breadcrumbs and the remaining cheese. Microwave on HIGH for 4–5 minutes until well heated through and the cheese has melted. Garnish it with parsley just before serving.

Serves 4 as a snack.

RATATOUILLE

2 aubergines, sliced
salt and pepper
30 ml (2 tbsp) vegetable oil
2 onions, skinned and sliced
2 courgettes, sliced
1 small green pepper, seeded and sliced
4 tomatoes, skinned, quartered and seeded
10 ml (2 tsp) chopped fresh basil or 2.5 ml
  (½ level tsp) dried
1 garlic clove, skinned and crushed
fresh basil sprigs, to garnish
garlic bread, to serve (see page 97)

1 Put the aubergine slices into a colander or sieve and sprinkle them with salt. Leave them to stand for 30 minutes, then rinse and drain the slices well on absorbent kitchen paper.

2 Put the oil and onions into a 2.8 litre (5 pint) ovenproof glass bowl. Cover them with cling film, pulling back one corner to vent, and microwave on HIGH for 5–7 minutes, stirring occasionally, until the onions soften.

3 Add the remaining vegetables, mint and garlic to the onions and mix well. Three-quarters cover with cling film and microwave on HIGH for 20–22 minutes until the vegetables are very soft, stirring two or three times during the cooking time.

4 Season the ratatouille well with salt and pepper. Allow it to cool, then cover it and refrigerate it for 3–4 hours, or overnight, until well chilled.

5 Serve the ratatouille in individual bowls, garnished with sprigs of basil, with hot garlic bread.

Serves 6 as a starter, 4 as a snack.

COURGETTE QUICHE

20.5 cm (8 inch) precooked pastry flan case
2 eggs, size 2
150 ml (¼ pint) milk
150 ml (¼ pint) single cream
50 g (2 oz) Cheddar cheese, grated
225 g (8 oz) courgettes, thinly sliced
salt and pepper

1 Lightly whisk together the eggs, milk and cream. Stir in the cheese and courgettes and season well with salt and pepper.

2 Place the pastry flan case on a large, flat ovenproof plate and carefully pour in the egg mixture.

3 Microwave the flan on MEDIUM for 18–19 minutes, giving the dish a quarter turn three times during cooking, until the filling is just beginning to set. Leave the quiche to stand for 10–15 minutes until completely set.

Serves 4–6.

QUICK PIZZA

226 g (8 oz) can tomatoes, well drained
10 ml (2 level tsp) tomato purée
2.5 ml (½ level tsp) dried mixed herbs or oregano
salt and pepper
225 g (8 oz) self-raising flour
60 ml (4 tbsp) vegetable oil
75–90 ml (5–6 tbsp) water
100 g (4 oz) Cheddar cheese, grated
a few anchovy fillets and stuffed green or black olives, to
  garnish

1 Put the tomatoes into a small bowl with the tomato purée, herbs, salt and pepper and mash well with a fork.

2 Put the flour and a pinch of salt into a mixing bowl, make a well in the centre, add the oil and water and mix together to form a soft dough. Knead it lightly on a floured surface until it is smooth.

3 Roll out the dough to two 20 cm (8 inch) rounds. Lightly oil two large, flat ovenproof plates and place a round of dough on each plate. Microwave the dough, one piece at a time, on HIGH for 2–3 minutes, or until the surface looks puffy.

4 Spread the mashed tomatoes over the two pieces of dough, then sprinkle them with the cheese. Garnish with anchovy fillets and olives.

5 Microwave the pizzas, one at a time, on HIGH for 4–5 minutes. Remove from the oven and leave it to stand for 3–4 minutes before serving.

Serves 2 as a snack.

SEAFOOD SCALLOPS

225 g (18 oz) haddock fillet
150 ml (¼ pint) dry white wine
small piece of onion
1 fresh parsley sprig
1 bay leaf
450 g (1 lb) potatoes, peeled and roughly chopped
75 g (3 oz) butter or margarine
225 g (8 fl oz) milk
salt and pepper
50 g (2 oz) button mushrooms, thinly sliced
45 ml (3 level tbsp) flour
50 g (2 oz) peeled prawns
chopped fresh parsley, to garnish

1 Place the haddock in a shallow ovenproof dish, pour over the wine and add the onion, parsley and bay leaf. Cover the dish with cling film, pulling back one corner to vent. Microwave on HIGH for 4–5 minutes until the fish is tender enough to flake easily.

2 Drain the haddock juices into a measuring jug and make it up to 150 ml (¼ pint) with water, if necessary. Skin and flake the fish. Set the fish and the cooking liquid aside.

3 Put the potatoes into a 1.7 litre (3 pint) ovenproof glass bowl and add 175 ml (15 tbsp) water. Three-quarters cover the bowl with cling film and microwave on HIGH for 6–8 minutes until the potatoes are cooked, stirring twice during the cooking time. Drain the potatoes well, then mash them with 40 g (1½ oz) of the butter, 25 ml (1 fl oz) milk and salt and pepper. Beat the potatoes until they are smooth and creamy.

4 Put 15 g (½ oz) of the remaining butter in a small ovenproof glass bowl, microwave on HIGH for 30 seconds until the butter melts, then stir in the mushrooms. Cover with cling film, pulling back one corner to vent, and microwave on HIGH for 2–3 minutes until the mushrooms are cooked, shaking the bowl two or three times during the cooking time.

5 Put the remaining butter into an ovenproof glass bowl and microwave on HIGH for 45 seconds until the butter melts. Stir in the flour and microwave on HIGH for 30 seconds, then gradually whisk in the remaining milk and the reserved fish liquid. Microwave on HIGH for 45 seconds, then whisk well. Microwave on HIGH for 2 minutes, whisking every 30 seconds until the sauce thickens. Season it well with salt and pepper. Stir in the flaked haddock, the mushrooms and the prawns.

6 Spoon the fish mixture into scallop shells or small gratin dishes. Put the potato in a large piping bag fitted with a large star nozzle and pipe a neat potato border around each scallop shell or gratin dish. Microwave on HIGH for about 5 minutes until the scallops are well heated through, changing the position of the scallops twice during the cooking time.

7 Garnish the scallops with parsley and serve them immediately. If wished, the scallops may be quickly browned under a hot grill just before serving.

Serves 4 as a starter.

WELSH RAREBIT

25 g (1 oz) butter or margarine
5 ml (1 level tsp) mustard powder
pinch of salt
pinch of cayenne pepper
dash of Worcestershire sauce
75 g (3 oz) mature Cheddar cheese, grated
30 ml (2 tbsp) brown ale
2 slices of bread, toasted

1 Place the butter in a small ovenproof glass bowl and microwave on HIGH for 30 seconds to soften.

2 Add the mustard powder, seasonings, Worcestershire sauce, grated cheese and ale and mix well.

3 Microwave on HIGH for about 30 seconds.

4 Beat well and spread the mixture over the toast. Place each slice on a serving plate and microwave the Welsh rarebit on HIGH for 20–30 seconds until hot. Serve immediately.

Serves 2.

STUFFED BAKED POTATOES

2 large potatoes, about 225 g (8 oz) each
25 g (1 oz) butter or margarine
1 small onion, skinned and finely chopped
30 ml (2 tbsp) milk
75 g (3 oz) Cheddar cheese, grated
30 ml (2 tbsp) chopped fresh parsley
salt and pepper

1 Scrub the potatoes thoroughly, then prick them all over using a fork. Microwave on HIGH for 10 minutes or until soft.

2 Place the butter in a medium ovenproof glass bowl and microwave on HIGH for 30 seconds or until melted. Add the onion and mix thoroughly. Three-quarters cover with cling film and microwave on HIGH for 5–7 minutes or until the onion is soft.

3 Halve the potatoes and scoop out the insides, leaving a thin shell. Add the potato flesh to the onion and mash well together.

4 Add the milk, half of the cheese and the parsley. Season to taste. Mix well together.

5 Pile the mixture back into the potato shells and place them on a large ovenproof serving dish. Sprinkle with the remaining cheese and microwave on HIGH for 2 minutes or until heated through.

6 Brown under a preheated grill if desired.

Serves 2.

BACON AND EGG SCRAMBLE

4 slices streaky bacon, rinded
4 eggs, beaten
30 ml (2 tbsp) double cream (optional)
25 g (1 oz) butter, cut into small pieces
salt and pepper
4 slices of bread, toasted
15 ml (1 tbsp) chopped fresh parsley

1 Snip the bacon fat at intervals to prevent curling. Place on an ovenproof plate and cover with absorbent kitchen paper.

2 Microwave on HIGH for 2–2½ minutes or until cooked. Chop roughly.

3 Place the eggs, cream, if using, and butter in a medium ovenproof glass bowl and season well with salt and pepper.

4 Microwave on HIGH for 1 minute, stirring well after 30 seconds. Add the bacon and microwave on HIGH for 1–1½ minutes or until the eggs are just cooked, stirring frequently.

5 Spoon the bacon and egg scramble on to toast, garnish with parsley and serve immediately.

Serves 2.

DEVILLED KIDNEYS

225 g (8 oz) lamb's kidneys
15 g (½ oz) butter or margarine
1 medium onion, skinned and chopped
1 garlic clove, skinned and crushed (optional)
2 rashers streaky bacon, chopped
5 ml (1 level tsp) cornflour
227 g (8 oz) can tomatoes
5 ml (1 level tsp) French mustard
5 ml (1 level tsp) tomato purée
2.5 ml (½ tsp) Worcestershire sauce
2.5 ml (½ level tsp) cayenne pepper
salt and pepper
French bread, to serve

1 Skin the kidneys and cut them in half. Remove the core with scissors or a sharp knife.

2 Put the butter in a large ovenproof glass bowl and microwave on HIGH for 30 seconds or until melted. Stir in the onion, garlic, if using, and bacon and microwave on HIGH for 5–7 minutes or until softened.

3 Blend the cornflour to a smooth paste with a little of the tomato juice. Add to the onion and garlic mixture with the remaining tomatoes and juice, mustard, tomato purée, Worcestershire sauce, cayenne pepper and seasoning.

4 Microwave on HIGH for 5–7 minutes until boiling and thickened, stirring occasionally.

5 Add the kidneys, cover with cling film and microwave on HIGH for 3½–4½ minutes or until the kidneys are cooked, stirring occasionally. Serve hot with French bread.

Serves 2.

POULTRY

Poultry of all kinds cooks well in the microwave either whole or cut into pieces. The only exception is turkey – large ones which weigh more than about 5.6 kg (12 lb) are difficult to turn and will cook unevenly.

When cooking poultry it is essential to ensure that it is properly thawed first. When thawing is complete the bird needs to stand for 10–15 minutes (30 minutes for large birds) before cooking. Do not cook boiling fowl in a microwave because the cooking process is too fast and the meat will be tough.

Whole chickens and turkeys are best cooked in a roasting bag loosely tied with string or an elastic band. Chickens may be cooked on a Low, Medium or High setting depending on how quickly you want them done. In general, lower settings produce more tender meat. If cooking chickens on High usually their leg and wing tips need to be protected with small pieces of foil to prevent them from drying out. If the chicken is not cooked in a roasting bag, it should be started breast side down so that the breast does not overcook and become dry while the rest of the bird is cooking.

When cooking chicken pieces it is best to remove the skin first. This will speed up the cooking time, prevent a fatty layer forming on the surface of the finished dish and allow the flavours of the other ingredients to penetrate the flesh. If you do not want to skin the chicken pieces and prefer them to have brown skins, first brown them either on the browning dish (see page 16) or in a frying pan on the hob.

To check if poultry is done it is best to use a meat thermometer – either the special microwave type which is left in the oven while the bird is cooking or an ordinary meat thermometer which should be checked after it has been removed from the oven. Letting the bird stand for 15–20 minutes suitably tented in foil will finish its cooking by raising the internal temperature by 5–6°C (10–15°F).

DEFROSTING POULTRY AND GAME

Poultry or game should be thawed in its freezer wrapping which should be pierced first and the metal tag removed. During defrosting, pour off liquid that collects in the bag. Finish defrosting in a bowl of cold water with the bird still in its bag. Chicken portions can be thawed in their polystyrene trays.

Type	Approximate time on LOW setting	Special instructions
Whole chicken or duckling	6–8 minutes per 450 g (1 lb)	Remove giblets. *Stand* in cold water for 30 minutes.
Whole turkey	10–12 minutes per 450 g (1 lb)	Remove giblets. *Stand* in cold water for 2–3 hours.
Chicken portions	5–7 minutes per 450 g (1 lb)	*Separate* during defrosting. *Stand* for 10 minutes.
Poussin, grouse, pheasant, pigeon, quail	5–7 minutes per 450 g (1 lb)	

TIME AND SETTINGS FOR COOKING POULTRY

Type	Time/Setting	Microwave Cooking Technique(s)
CHICKEN		
Whole chicken	8–10 minutes on HIGH per 450 g (1 lb)	*Cook* in a roasting bag, breast side down and turn halfway through cooking. *Brown* under conventional grill, if preferred. *Stand* for 10–15 minutes.
Whole poussin	5 minutes on HIGH	*Cook* in a pierced roasting bag. *Turn* over as for whole chicken.
Portions	6–8 minutes on HIGH per 450 g (1 lb)	*Position* skin side up with thinner parts towards the centre. *Re-position* halfway through cooking time. *Stand* for 5–10 minutes.
Boneless breast	2–3 minutes on HIGH	*Brown* under grill, if preferred.
DUCK		
Whole	7–10 minutes on HIGH per 450 g (1 lb)	*Turn* over as for whole chicken. *Stand* for 10–15 minutes.
Portions	4 × 300 g (11 oz) pieces: 10 minutes on HIGH, then 30–35 minutes on MEDIUM	*Position* and *re-position* as for chicken portions above.
TURKEY		
Whole	9–11 minutes on HIGH per 450 g (1 lb)	*Turn* over 3–4 times, depending on size, during cooking; start cooking breast side down. *Stand* for 10–15 minutes.
Boneless roll	10 minutes on HIGH per 450 g (1 lb)	*Turn* over halfway through cooking time.

MARINATED CHICKEN WITH PEANUT SAUCE

60 ml (4 tbsp) olive oil
30 ml (2 tbsp) herb vinegar
10 ml (2 level tsp) Dijon mustard
grated rind and juice of ½ a lemon
15 ml (1 tbsp) soy sauce
1 garlic clove, skinned and crushed
salt and pepper
4 chicken breast fillets, skinned

For the sauce:
1 small onion, skinned and chopped
2 large tomatoes, skinned and chopped
1 garlic clove, skinned and chopped
15 ml (1 level tbsp) tomato purée
1.25–2.5 ml (¼–½ level tsp) cayenne pepper
75 ml (3 fl oz) chicken stock
15 ml (1 tbsp) soy sauce
60 ml (4 level tbsp) peanut butter
slices of lemon and lime, to garnish

1 To make the marinade, whisk together the oil, vinegar, mustard, lemon rind and juice, soy sauce, garlic and seasonings until well blended.

2 Cut the chicken into 2.5 cm (1 inch) cubes and thread these on to 8 wooden kebab sticks. Place these in a shallow ovenproof dish and pour the marinade over. Cover with cling film, pulling back one corner to vent. Leave to stand for 2 hours or overnight.

3 In a blender or food processor blend all the ingredients for the sauce until smooth. Pour the sauce into an ovenproof glass bowl, cover and set aside until it is needed.

4 Place the covered chicken in the oven and microwave on HIGH for about 10–12 minutes, or until the chicken is cooked, turning and re-positioning at least twice during the cooking time.

5 Arrange the chicken in a serving dish. Reserve the cooking liquid and keep it hot while heating the sauce.

6 Add the reserved cooking liquid to the sauce mixture, cover with cling film and microwave on HIGH for 5–6 minutes, until boiling, stirring frequently.

7 Garnish the chicken with slices of lemon and lime. Pour the sauce into a serving jug or bowl and serve it separately with the chicken.

Serves 4.

CHICKEN FRICASSEE

Roast the chicken first before cutting it into large pieces and finishing it in the coriander sauce. Alternatively, use about 350 g (12 oz) left-over cooked chicken or turkey flesh.

1.4 kg (3 lb) oven-ready roasting chicken
25 g (1 oz) butter or margarine
salt and pepper
225 g (8 oz) carrots, peeled and thinly sliced
45 ml (3 tbsp) vegetable oil
45 ml (3 level tbsp) plain flour
300 ml (½ pint) chicken stock
45 ml (3 tbsp) chopped fresh coriander leaves
425 g (15 oz) can chick-peas
chopped fresh coriander, to garnish

1 Place the chicken breast side down in a 2.3 litre (4 pint) microwave dish and spread it with the butter. Next, sprinkle it with pepper.

2 Cover the chicken loosely with greaseproof paper and microwave on HIGH for 6 minutes per 450 g (1 lb); leave it to stand for 15 minutes.

3 Cut all the flesh off the bone and divide it into pieces. Reserve the skin and bones for stock, if wished.

4 Place the carrots in a casserole dish with the oil. Cover and microwave on HIGH for 4 minutes.

5 Stir in the flour, followed by the stock, the seasonings and the coriander leaves. Add the chicken and the drained chick-peas, stirring well to mix.

6 Cover and microwave on HIGH for 4 minutes, then stir well. Re-cover and microwave on HIGH for a further 4 minutes.

7 Leave the chicken to stand for 5 minutes. Adjust the seasoning, garnish with fresh coriander and serve.

Serves 4.

CHICKEN WITH APPLE AND CIDER

3 large red-skinned eating apples
15 ml (1 tbsp) vegetable oil
50 g (2 oz) butter or margarine
4 chicken leg portions, skinned
1 small onion, skinned and sliced
10 ml (2 level tsp) paprika
15 ml (1 level tbsp) plain flour
300 ml (½ pint) chicken stock
150 ml (¼ pint) sweet cider
salt and pepper

1 Quarter and core 1 of the eating apples, then halve each quarter lengthwise.

2 Preheat a large browning dish according to the manufacturer's instructions, adding the oil and the butter for the last 30 seconds. (Or, put the oil and the butter into a large shallow ovenproof casserole and microwave on HIGH for 1–2 minutes until hot).

3 Without removing the dish from the oven, put the apple pieces into the browning dish, turning the pieces in the oil and butter mixture to coat and brown them evenly. Microwave on HIGH for 1 minute. Remove the apple pieces from the dish and set them aside.

4 Place the chicken portions in the browning dish and microwave on HIGH for 4 minutes, turning them over after 3 minutes. Remove the chicken portions from the dish and set them aside.

5 Peel, core and slice the remaining eating apples. Stir, with the onion, into the fat remaining in the cooking dish and microwave on HIGH for 2–3 minutes, stirring twice during the cooking time.

6 Stir in the paprika and flour and microwave on HIGH for 1 minute, stirring twice. Add the stock and cider. Return the chicken portions to the dish, spooning the sauce over them. Season well with salt and pepper. Cover the dish with a lid, or with cling film, pulling back one corner to vent.

7 Microwave the chicken on HIGH for 10 minutes, then reduce the setting and microwave on LOW for 25–30 minutes until the chicken portions are very tender. Re-position the chicken portions three or four times during the cooking time.

8 Cover and leave it to stand for 10 minutes. Garnish the chicken with the reserved apple pieces before serving.

Serves 4.

CHICKEN WITH MUSHROOMS AND FENNEL

1 350 g (12 oz) bulb Florence fennel
1 medium onion, skinned and sliced
45 ml (3 tbsp) vegetable oil
125 g (4 oz) button mushrooms, quartered
45 ml (3 level tbsp) plain flour
150 ml (¼ pint) dry white wine
300 ml (½ pint) chicken stock
salt and pepper
4 chicken leg portions, about 800 g (1¾ lb), skinned and cut in half
chopped fresh parsley, to garnish

1 Slice the fennel into thin even-sized pieces and place it in a 2.3 litre (4 pint) microwave dish with the oil. Cover and microwave on HIGH for 6 minutes.

2 Stir the flour into the casserole and microwave on HIGH for 1 minute. Add the wine, stock, seasonings, chicken and mushrooms, ensuring that they are covered by the liquid.

3 Cover and microwave on HIGH for 8 minutes. Stir well, re-cover and microwave on HIGH for a further 8 minutes.

4 Leave the chicken to stand for 5 minutes. Adjust the seasoning and serve garnished with chopped parsley.

Serves 4.

CHICKEN WITH VEGETABLE SAUCE

50 g (2 oz) butter or margarine
3 carrots, peeled and finely chopped
2 leeks, white parts only, trimmed, washed and thinly sliced
2 celery sticks, washed, trimmed and thinly sliced
6 chicken breasts
600 ml (1 pint) boiling chicken stock
25 g (1 oz) flour
150 ml (¼ pint) double cream
1 egg yolk
5 ml (1 tsp) lemon juice
salt and pepper
nutmeg
100 g (4 oz) Comté or Gruyère cheese, grated

1 Put 25 g (1 oz) of the butter into a large ovenproof casserole. Microwave on HIGH for 1 minute until the butter melts. Add the carrots, leeks and celery, stir well and cover with a lid or cling film and microwave on HIGH for 10 minutes until the vegetables are softened, stirring twice.

2 Arrange the chicken on top of the vegetables. Pour in the boiling chicken stock. Cover and microwave on HIGH for 10–15 minutes, or until the chicken is tender, giving the dish a quarter turn three times during cooking.

3 Carefully lift the chicken from the casserole and place it in a large shallow ovenproof dish; cover and keep the chicken warm.

4 Strain the liquid from the casserole, reserving 600 ml (1 pint), making it up to the right quantity with more stock, if necessary.

5 Put the vegetables in a food processor or blender to form a purée, then mix this with the reserved stock.

6 Mix together the remaining butter and the flour to make a beurre manié.

7 Microwave the vegetable and stock mixture on HIGH for about 5 minutes until it is hot but not boiling. Gradually whisk in the beurre manié, a few pieces at a time, until it is all incorporated. Microwave on HIGH for 4–5 minutes until boiling and whisk well.

8 Stir the cream into the egg yolk and stir in the lemon juice to make a smooth sauce. Gradually whisk the cream and egg mixture into this. Season well with salt, pepper and a little grated nutmeg.

9 Sprinkle half of the cheese over the chicken breasts and press it down firmly.

10 Pour enough sauce to cover the chicken and sprinkle with the remaining cheese.

11 Microwave on HIGH for 4–5 minutes until the cheese melts and the sauce and chicken are hot. Brown under a hot grill and serve immediately with the remaining sauce passed separately.

Serves 6.

CHICKEN LIVER BOLOGNESE

50 g (2 oz) butter or margarine
2 medium onions, skinned and chopped
125 g (4 oz) carrot, peeled and finely chopped
125 g (4 oz) celery, washed, trimmed and finely chopped
125 g (4 oz) streaky bacon, rinded and chopped
450 g (1 lb) chicken livers, prepared and chopped
150 ml (¼ pint) red wine
30 ml (1 level tbsp) tomato purée
150 ml (¼ pint) beef stock
2.5 ml (½ level tsp) dried oregano
1 bay leaf
salt and pepper
spaghetti, to serve (see page 85)

1 Put the butter into a shallow ovenproof casserole and microwave on HIGH for 1 minute until the butter melts. Stir in the vegetables, and cover them with a lid, or with cling film, pulling back one corner to vent. Microwave on HIGH for 5–6 minutes until the vegetables are softened.

2 Uncover the dish, stir in the bacon and livers and microwave on HIGH for 3–4 minutes, stirring twice.

3 Add the wine, tomato purée, stock, oregano and bay leaf to the chicken livers, season well with salt and pepper and stir well. Microwave on HIGH for 1 minute until boiling. Boil for 1 minute, stirring twice. Cover the dish with a lid, or with cling film, pulling back one corner to vent. Microwave on HIGH for 8 minutes, stirring twice. Serve the Bolognese poured over hot, buttered spaghetti.

Serves 4.

SPANISH CHICKEN

15 ml (1 tbsp) vegetable oil
15 g (½ oz) butter or margarine
4 chicken joints
397 g (14 oz) can tomatoes
1 Spanish onion, skinned and finely sliced
1 red pepper, seeded and sliced
1 green pepper, seeded and sliced
2.5 ml (½ level tsp) dried basil
salt and pepper
15 ml (1 level tbsp) cornflour

1 Preheat a browning dish to maximum, according to the manufacturer's instructions, adding the oil and butter for the last 15 seconds. (Or, put the oil and butter into a large shallow ovenproof casserole and microwave on HIGH for 1–2 minutes until hot.)

2 Without removing the dish from the oven, quickly place the chicken pieces, skin side down, in the hot fat. Microwave on HIGH for 3 minutes, then turn the pieces over.

3 Push the tomatoes, with their juice, through a sieve. Stir this into the chicken with the onion, peppers, basil and seasonings. Cover with the lid or cling film and continue to cook on HIGH for 12 minutes, re-positioning the chicken twice during the cooking time.

4 Reduce the setting to LOW and cook for a further 10 minutes, or until the chicken is tender.

5 Remove the pieces to a warmed serving dish. Blend the cornflour to a paste with a little cold water and stir this into the juices. Microwave on HIGH for 5 minutes, stirring once. Pour over the chicken and serve.

Serves 4.

CHICKEN AND COCONUT CURRY

50 g (2 oz) desiccated coconut
200 ml (7 fl oz) milk
30 ml (2 tbsp) vegetable oil
4 celery sticks, washed, trimmed and sliced
1 medium onion, skinned and sliced
1 large red pepper, seeded and sliced
225 g (8 oz) cooking apples, peeled, cored and sliced
2.5 ml (½ level tsp) chilli powder
5 ml (1 level tsp) ground cinnamon
60 ml (4 level tbsp) plain flour
1.8 kg (4 lb) chicken, boned, skinned and the flesh cut
  into 2.5 cm (1 inch) cubes
450 ml (¾ pint) chicken stock
salt and pepper
coriander leaves or parsley, to garnish

1 Put the coconut and milk into an ovenproof glass bowl and microwave on HIGH for 3–4 minutes until boiling. Remove this from the oven, cover and leave the milk to infuse for 30 minutes.

2 Strain the milk through a fine sieve into another bowl, pressing the coconut to extract all the juices, then reserve.

3 Put the oil into a large ovenproof casserole with the celery, onion, red pepper and apple and mix the ingredients together well. Cover the dish with a lid, or with cling film, pulling back one corner to vent. Microwave on HIGH for 5–6 minutes until the vegetables soften.

4 Uncover the dish and stir in the spices and the flour and microwave on HIGH for 2 minutes. Arrange the chicken pieces on top of the vegetables and microwave on HIGH for 4–5 minutes until the pieces of chicken become opaque, turning over the pieces during the cooking time.

5 Pour the stock and coconut milk over the chicken and season it with salt and pepper. Stir well, then cover with a lid, or with cling film, pulling back one corner to vent. Microwave on HIGH for 6–8 minutes until boiling. Reduce the setting and microwave on LOW for 20–30 minutes until the chicken is very tender.

6 Leave it to stand for 5 minutes and sprinkle with coriander leaves or parsley just before serving.

Serves 4.

STUFFED ROAST CHICKEN

30 ml (2 tbsp) vegetable oil
1 small onion, skinned and chopped
25 g (1 oz) dried apricots
50 g (2 oz) fresh brown breadcrumbs
25 g (1 oz) salted cashew nuts
2.5 ml (½ level tsp) dried rosemary
2.5 ml (½ level tsp) lemon rind
salt and pepper
a little beaten egg
about 1.4 kg (3 lb) oven-ready roasting chicken
25 g (1 oz) butter or margarine
paprika
10 ml (2 level tsp) plain flour

1 To prepare the stuffing, put the oil in an ovenproof glass bowl and microwave on HIGH for 1 minute. Add the onion and microwave on HIGH for 4–5 minutes until soft.

2 Snip the apricots into small pieces and stir them into the bowl with the breadcrumbs, chopped nuts, rosemary, lemon rind and the seasonings.

3 Add sufficient beaten egg to form a soft stuffing.

4 Fill the neck end of the bird with the stuffing.

5 Tie the chicken legs together with string. Spread the butter over the bird and sprinkle it lightly with paprika. Sprinkle the flour inside a roasting bag and then place the chicken inside. Tie the bag loosely with string, making sure there is room for the steam to escape.

6 Weigh the bird and then place it in a shallow microwave dish. Microwave on MEDIUM for 9 minutes per 450 g (1 lb).

7 Leave the chicken to stand for about 15 minutes before unwrapping it. Carve the bird and serve it accompanied by the cooking juices.

Serves 4.

CHICKEN BREASTS STUFFED WITH STILTON

125 g (4 oz) Stilton cheese, crumbled
75 g (3 oz) unsalted butter, softened
4 chicken breasts, skinned and boned
8 rashers smoked back bacon, rinded
45 ml (3 tbsps) vegetable oil
100 ml (4 fl oz) red wine made up to 300 ml (½ pint)
*   with chicken stock*
10 ml (2 level tsp) arrowroot
salt and pepper
watercress, to garnish

1 Cream the Stilton and unsalted butter together to make a smooth paste.

2 Flatten the chicken breasts between two sheets of greaseproof paper. Make a horizontal slit in the centre of each breast to make a pocket and fill the pockets with the Stilton butter. Wind the bacon rashers around each breast.

3 Heat a browning dish according to the manufacturer's instructions, adding the oil and butter for the last 30 seconds. (Or, put the butter and oil into a shallow ovenproof dish and microwave on HIGH for 2 minutes until hot.)

4 Without removing the browning dish from the oven, place the chicken breasts in the dish rounded sides down. Microwave on HIGH for 5 minutes, turning the chicken over halfway during cooking.

5 Pour the wine and stock into the dish, microwave on HIGH for about 5 minutes until boiling. Cover the dish with a lid or with cling film, pulling back one corner to vent. Reduce the setting to LOW and microwave for about 10 minutes until the chicken is very tender.

6 Lift the chicken breasts from the dish, place on a hot serving dish, cover and keep warm.

7 Blend the arrowroot with a little cold water to a smooth paste and stir this into the cooking juices. Microwave on HIGH for 4–5 minutes until the sauce thickens. Season well with salt and pepper.

8 Pour the sauce over the chicken breasts, garnish with watercress and serve.

Serves 4.

CHICKEN HOT-POT

1.4 kg (3 lb) oven-ready roasting chicken
2 medium onions, skinned and sliced
439 g (15½ oz) can butter beans
700 g (1½ lb) floury potatoes, peeled and sliced
salt and pepper
450 ml (¾ pint) chicken stock
10 ml (2 level tsp) Dijon mustard
15 ml (1 level tbsp) tomato purée
25 g (1 oz) butter or margarine
chopped parsley, to garnish

1 Remove all the flesh from the chicken and discard the skin and bone. Dice it into 2.5 cm (1 inch) pieces, including any scraps.

2 Layer up the chicken, onions and drained beans with one-third of the potatoes in a 2.4 litre (4½ pint) ovenproof casserole, seasoning each layer well with salt and pepper.

3 Mix the stock with the mustard and tomato purée and pour the mixture into the dish. Overlap the rest of the potatoes neatly on top and dot with the butter.

4 Cover the dish with a lid or with cling film, pulling back one corner to vent. Microwave on HIGH for about 10 minutes until the stock comes to the boil. Reduce the setting and microwave on LOW for 30–40 minutes until the potatoes and chicken are cooked.

5 Brown the hot-pot under a hot grill, sprinkle parsley over the top and serve.

Serves 4.

CHICKEN PAPRIKA

50 g (2 oz) butter or margarine
2 large onions, skinned and sliced
1 garlic clove, skinned and crushed
15 ml (1 level tbsp) paprika
2.5 ml (½ level tsp) cayenne pepper
25 g (1 oz) plain flour
45 ml (3 level tbsp) tomato purée
450 ml (¾ pint) chicken stock
salt and pepper
4 chicken leg portions, skinned and cut in half
150 ml (¼ pint) natural yogurt
chopped fresh parsley, to garnish

1 Place the butter in a large ovenproof casserole and microwave on HIGH for 45 seconds until the butter melts, then stir in the onions and garlic. Cover with a lid or with cling film, pulling back one corner to vent. Microwave on HIGH for 5–6 minutes until the onions soften.

2 Stir the paprika and cayenne pepper into the onions and microwave on HIGH for 30 seconds. Stir in the flour and microwave on HIGH for 1 minute. Add the tomato purée, stock, seasonings and the chicken pieces and cover with a lid or with cling film, pulling back one corner to vent. Microwave on HIGH for 25 minutes, or until the chicken is cooked. Turn and re-position the pieces at least twice during the cooking time.

3 Use a slotted draining spoon to transfer the chicken to a plate; cover and keep warm.

4 Stir the yogurt into the sauce and adjust the seasoning, then microwave on HIGH for 3–4 minutes until hot but not boiling. Return the chicken pieces to the casserole and microwave on HIGH for 1 minute. Serve garnished with chopped parsley.

Serves 4.

SWEET AND SOUR CHICKEN

450 g (1 lb) chicken breast, skinned
75 g (3 oz) soft brown sugar
75 ml (5 tbsp) wine vinegar
45 ml (3 tbsp) soy sauce
45 ml (3 level tbsp) cornflour
1 green pepper, seeded and thinly sliced
225 g (8 oz) carrots, peeled and cut into thin strips
397 g (14 oz) can tomatoes
50 g (2 oz) beansprouts

1 Cut the chicken into 2.5 cm (1 inch) strips.

2 In a large casserole, blend together the sugar, vinegar, soy sauce and cornflour. Microwave on HIGH for 3 minutes or until just boiling, stirring occasionally.

3 Stir in the green pepper, carrots, tomatoes and juice, and add the chicken. Cover and microwave on HIGH for 5 minutes until boiling, then continue microwaving on HIGH for 12–15 minutes or until the chicken is tender, stirring occasionally.

4 Add the beansprouts and microwave, uncovered, on HIGH for 2 minutes. Serve with boiled rice (see page 85).

Serves 4.

CHICKEN SALAD

1.4 kg (3 lb) oven-ready roasting chicken
1 Iceberg or Webb lettuce, washed and shredded
225 g (8 oz) Emmental cheese, diced
2 eggs, hard-boiled and quartered
6 small tomatoes, halved, or 2 large tomatoes, quartered
3 spring onions, washed, trimmed and finely chopped
90 ml (6 tbsp) olive or vegetable oil
45 ml (3 tbsp) wine vinegar or lemon juice
2.5 ml (½ tsp) sugar
2.5 ml (½ tsp) wholegrain, Dijon or French mustard
salt and pepper
1 garlic clove, skinned and crushed
30 ml (2 tbsp) finely chopped fresh parsley

1 Remove any excess fat from inside the chicken. Place the chicken in a roasting bag, breast side up. Tie the end of the bag loosely with a plastic tie or an elastic band, leaving a gap for steam to escape.

2 Microwave the chicken on MEDIUM for 27 minutes or until the chicken is cooked. It is done when there is no sign of pink flesh, and the juices run clear when the chicken is pierced with the tip of a knife at the thickest part of the thigh.

3 Allow the chicken to cool in the roasting bag, then remove all the meat from the bones, discarding the skin. Cut the meat into neat strips.

4 Line a serving dish with the shredded lettuce, then arrange the chicken and cheese alternately around the edge of the dish. Add the eggs and the tomatoes and sprinkle the finely chopped spring onions over the top.

5 Place the oil, vinegar, sugar, mustard, salt and pepper, garlic and parsley in a bowl or screw-top jar and whisk or shake together. Pour it into a serving jug and serve the dressing separately with the salad.

Serves 4.

SAUTEED TURKEY AND BANANA WITH LEMON SAUCE

900 g (2 lb) turkey breast
25 g (1 oz) seasoned flour
25 g (1 oz) butter or margarine
100 g (4 oz) streaky bacon, rinded and chopped
300 ml (½ pint) chicken stock
salt and pepper
3 bananas
45 ml (3 tbsp) lemon juice
watercress and lemon slices, to garnish

1 Cut the turkey meat into neat strips about 1 cm (½ inch) wide and 7.5 cm (3 inches) long. Toss them in the seasoned flour.

2 Preheat a large browning dish according to the manufacturer's instructions, adding the butter for the last 30 seconds. (Or, put the butter in a large shallow ovenproof dish and microwave on HIGH for 1–2 minutes until the butter is hot.)

3 Without removing the dish from the oven, add the turkey strips and the bacon to the hot butter, stirring them quickly in the butter to coat and brown them evenly. Cover with a lid, or cling film, pulling back one corner to vent. Microwave on HIGH for 12–15 minutes, stirring frequently during the cooking time. Add the lemon juice, stock and seasonings and stir well. Microwave on HIGH for 10 minutes, stirring frequently, until boiling.

4 Slice the bananas and stir them into the turkey. Microwave on HIGH uncovered for 1–2 minutes, stirring occasionally.

5 Serve garnished with watercress and lemon slices.

Serves 6.

TURKEY PAUPIETTES WITH CUMIN

8 thin turkey escalopes or 700 g (1½ lb) turkey fillet
salt and pepper
450 g (1 lb) pork sausagemeat or sausages, skinned
60 ml (4 level tbsp) mango chutney
50 g (2 oz) salted peanuts, chopped
25 g (1 oz) butter or margarine
30 ml (2 tbsp) vegetable oil
450 g (1 lb) parsnips, peeled and sliced
450 g (1 lb) onions, skinned and sliced
15 ml (1 level tbsp) ground cumin
45 ml (3 level tbsp) plain flour
45 ml (3 level tbsp) desiccated coconut
450 ml (¾ pint) chicken stock

1 Flatten the turkey escalopes or fillet between two sheets of greaseproof paper into eight thin pieces. Season them well.

2 Mix the sausagemeat with 30 ml (2 level tbsp) of the chutney, the nuts and seasoning. Divide the mixture among the escalopes. Roll them up and secure them with wooden cocktail sticks.

3 Put the butter and oil into a shallow ovenproof casserole and microwave on HIGH for 45 seconds until the butter melts. Add the parsnips and onions. Three-quarters cover with cling film and microwave on HIGH for 8–10 minutes until the vegetables have softened, stirring frequently.

4 Stir the cumin, flour and coconut into the parsnips and microwave on HIGH for 2 minutes. Stir in the stock and remaining chutney and season well with salt and pepper. Place the turkey paupiettes on top of the vegetables in a single layer. Cover the dish with a lid or cling film, pulling back one corner to vent.

5 Microwave on HIGH for 8 minutes until boiling, giving the dish a quarter turn three times during cooking. Reduce the setting and microwave on LOW for 25–30 minutes until the turkey is tender, giving the dish a quarter turn three times during cooking. Carefully remove the cocktail sticks and skim any excess fat from the surface. Cover and leave the turkey paupiettes to stand for 5–10 minutes before serving.

Serves 4.

SPICED TURKEY

450 g (1 lb) turkey fillet
5 ml (1 level tsp) paprika
5 ml (1 level tsp) ground cumin
5 ml (1 level tsp) ground coriander
pinch of ground ginger
pinch of ground cloves
5 ml (1 level tsp) ground cinnamon
150 ml (¼ pint) natural yogurt
15 ml (1 tbsp) vegetable oil
15 ml (1 level tbsp) plain flour
25 g (1 oz) ground almonds
1 garlic clove, skinned and crushed
salt and pepper

1 Cut the turkey into 2.5 cm (1 inch) strips and place in a large bowl. Add the paprika, cumin, coriander, ginger, cloves, cinnamon and yogurt. Mix thoroughly. Cover and leave to marinate for at least 1 hour.

2 Heat a browning dish to maximum according to the manufacturer's instructions, adding the oil for the last 30 seconds.

3 Add the flour and almonds and microwave on HIGH for 30 seconds. Stir in the turkey and marinade, garlic and seasoning, and mix together well.

4 Microwave on HIGH for 2 minutes, stirring occasionally, then cover and microwave on LOW for 20–25 minutes, or until the turkey is tender, stirring occasionally. Serve hot with boiled rice (see page 85) and poppadums.

Serves 4.

Lamb burgers – These quarter pounders, served in buns, with lettuce and tomato ketchup, are a favourite children's snack.
Recipe on page 58.

SHREDDED TURKEY WITH COURGETTES

450 g (1 lb) turkey or chicken breast fillets
450 g (1 lb) courgettes
1 red pepper, seeded and thinly sliced
45 ml (3 tbsp) vegetable oil
45 ml (3 tbsp) dry sherry
15 ml (1 tbsp) soy sauce
salt and pepper
60 ml (4 tbsp) natural yogurt or soured cream

1 Cut all the ingredients into fine strips to ensure even cooking.

2 Place all the ingredients except the yogurt in a 2.3 litre (4 pint) microwave dish, season and stir well to mix.

3 Cover with a lid or cling film and microwave on HIGH for 4 minutes.

4 Leave to stand for 5 minutes, then add the yogurt, adjust the seasoning and serve.

Serves 4.

TURKEY WITH MUSHROOMS AND YOGURT

450 g (1 lb) turkey breast, skinned
25 g (1 oz) butter or margarine
1 medium onion, skinned and chopped
25 g (1 oz) plain flour
300 ml (½ pint) milk
100 g (4 oz) mushrooms, sliced
salt and pepper
nutmeg
1.25 ml (¼ level tsp) ground ginger
150 ml (¼ pint) natural yogurt
2 egg yolks
lemon slices and chopped fresh parsley, to garnish

1 Cut the turkey into 2.5 cm (1 inch) cubes and put them in a small roasting bag. Loosely tie the end of the bag with a plastic tie or a rubber band. Microwave on HIGH for 6 minutes, or until the turkey is cooked.

2 Put the butter in an ovenproof casserole and microwave on HIGH for 45 seconds until it is melted, then stir in the onion. Cover with a lid or with cling film, pulling back one corner to vent. Microwave on HIGH for 5–7 minutes or until the onion softens.

3 Stir the flour into the onion and microwave on HIGH for 1 minute. Gradually stir in the milk. Microwave on HIGH for 45 seconds, then whisk. Continue to microwave on HIGH for 1¾–2 minutes, whisking every 30 seconds, until the sauce is boiling.

4 Add the turkey and any juices in the roasting bag and the mushrooms to the sauce. Season well with the salt, pepper, freshly grated nutmeg and ginger. Microwave on HIGH for 2–3 minutes, stirring once.

5 Blend the yogurt and egg yolks together until smooth and stir this into the turkey mixture. Microwave on HIGH for 1½–2 minutes until very hot but not boiling, stirring two or three times during the cooking time.

6 Serve the turkey garnished with the lemon slices and parsley.

Serves 4.

Sage and bacon-stuffed pork – is an easy dish to prepare and makes a delicious and satisfying meal.
Recipe on page 60.

STIR-FRIED TURKEY AND MANGE-TOUT

450 g (1 lb) turkey fillet
2.5 cm (1 inch) piece of fresh root ginger, grated
60 ml (4 tbsp) soy sauce
60 ml (4 tbsp) dry sherry
5 ml (1 level tsp) five-spice powder
1 garlic clove, skinned and crushed
30 ml (2 tbsp) vegetable oil
30 ml (2 level tbsp) cornflour
150 ml (¼ pint) chicken stock
salt and pepper
175 g (6 oz) mange-tout, trimmed
25 g (1 oz) cashew nuts (optional)
spring onion tassels, to garnish

1 Cut the turkey into 2.5 cm (1 inch) strips. Put these into a large bowl with the ginger, soy sauce, sherry, five-spice powder and garlic. Stir well, then cover and leave to marinate for at least 1 hour.

2 Heat a browning dish to maximum according to the manufacturer's instructions, adding the oil for the last 30 seconds.

3 Remove the turkey from the marinade with a slotted spoon and add it to the browning dish. Reserve the marinade. Quickly stir the turkey in the oil and microwave on HIGH for 2 minutes.

4 Meanwhile, blend the cornflour with the reserved marinade, then stir in the stock.

5 Add the marinade mixture to the turkey and mix thoroughly. Season and then stir in the mange-tout.

6 Microwave on HIGH for 4–5 minutes or until the turkey is tender, stirring occasionally.

7 Stir in the cashew nuts, if using, and microwave on HIGH for 1 minute.

8 Serve hot garnished with spring onion tassels.

Serves 4.

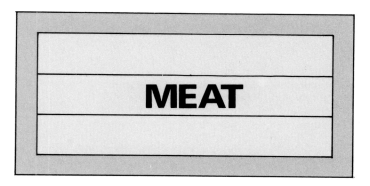

MEAT

Cooking meat in a microwave oven requires care as no two pieces of meat are ever identical. Cooking time will depend on the shape, density and starting temperature of each piece.

Microwave cooking does not take long enough to tenderise the cheaper coarse cuts of meat so casseroles made from these may be better prepared conventionally and then reheated in the microwave. If you do want to make this type of casserole in the microwave, it is best to make it in advance, allow it to cool and then reheat it when required. This gives the different flavours a better chance of mingling. Tough cuts can be improved if they are marinated before being microwaved.

When roasting a piece of meat choose a regular, compact shape that will cook evenly. Trim off any thick fat as this will attract microwaves and the meat near it will cook faster than the rest.

Microwaving draws fat out of meat and whilst this is useful for slimmers, it can prove a problem since microwaves are attracted to fat. When cooking fatty meat for a long period, stand the meat on a roasting rack or an upturned saucer to prevent the meat from re-absorbing any fat and, at regular intervals, remove the fat which collects below the meat to prevent a pool forming. Cook fatty mince in a plastic colander over a bowl to catch the fat as it drips out.

Large joints will brown because of the length of cooking time but small ones will not. If you like a brown finish, either put the meat under the grill or else briefly in a hot oven at the end of the cooking time. Other alternatives are to use a light brushing of soy sauce or gravy browning or to sprinkle the meat with brown or red spices or special microwave browning powder.

Meat roasted in a microwave shrinks less than when roasted conventionally. If left uncovered, it is more likely to brown, but it will tend to splatter the oven with fat. To avoid this, use a roasting bag tied with string or an elastic band, *not* a metal tie tag, and pierce the bag so that steam can escape. Stand the joint on a small roasting rack or upturned saucer in the bag so that it doesn't sit in a pool of fat.

When the roasting time is completed, remove the joint from the oven and cover it with a tent made from a piece of foil (shiny side in). After standing for about 15–20 minutes, the internal temperature of the meat will rise by about 5–7°C (10–15°F). To check whether or not the joint is done, push a meat thermometer into the thickest part of it and read the temperature. Some microwave ovens have a built-in temperature probe which you can read through the door while the meat is cooking – or you can buy one separately. Don't use a conventional meat thermometer inside the oven as the microwave energy will affect the mercury.

Never salt meat before cooking it in a microwave since salt attracts moisture and this affects the patterns of the microwaves.

DEFROSTING MEAT

Frozen meat exudes a lot of liquid during defrosting and because microwaves are attracted to water, the liquid should be poured off or mopped up with absorbent kitchen paper when it collects, otherwise defrosting will take longer. Start defrosting a joint in its wrapper and remove it as soon as possible – usually after one-quarter of the defrosting time. Place the joint on a microwave roasting rack so that it does not stand in liquid during defrosting.

Remember to turn over a large piece of meat. If the joint shows signs of cooking give the meat a 'rest' period of 20 minutes. Alternatively, shield the 'thin ends' or parts which will thaw more quickly with small, smooth pieces of foil. A joint is thawed when a skewer can easily pass through the thickest part of the meat. Chops and steaks should be re-positioned during defrosting; test them by pressing the surface with your fingers – the meat should feel cold to the touch and give in the thickest part.

Do not allow the foil used for shielding to touch the sides of the oven.

Type	Approximate time on LOW setting	Special instructions
BEEF		
Boned roasting joints (sirloin, topside)	8–10 minutes per 450 g (1 lb)	*Turn* over regularly during defrosting and rest if the meat shows signs of cooking. *Stand* for 1 hour.
Joints on bone (rib of beef)	10–12 minutes per 450 g (1 lb)	*Shield* bone end with small, smooth pieces of foil and overwrap it with cling film. *Turn* over joint during defrosting. The meat will still be icy in the centre but will complete thawing if you leave it to stand for 1 hour.
Minced beef	8–10 minutes per 450 g (1 lb)	*Stand* for 10 minutes.
Cubed steak	6–8 minutes per 450 g (1 lb)	*Stand* for 10 minutes.
Steak (sirloin, rump)	8–10 minutes per 450 g (1 lb)	*Stand* for 10 minutes.
Beefburgers standard (50 g/2 oz)	2 burgers: 2 minutes 4 burgers: 2–3 minutes	Can be cooked from frozen, without defrosting, if preferred.
quarter-pounder	2 burgers: 2–3 minutes 4 burgers: 5 minutes	
burger buns	2 buns: 2 minutes	*Stand* burger buns for 2 minutes.
LAMB/VEAL		
Boned rolled joint (loin, leg, shoulder)	5–6 minutes per 450 g (1 lb)	As for boned roasting joints of beef above. *Stand* for 30–45 minutes.
On the bone (leg and shoulder)	5–6 minutes per 450 g (1 lb)	As for beef joints on bone above. *Stand* for 30–45 minutes.
Minced lamb or veal	8–10 minutes per 450 g (1 lb)	*Stand* for 10 minutes.
Chops	8–10 minutes per 450 g (1 lb)	*Separate* during defrosting. *Stand* for 10 minutes.
PORK		
Boned rolled joint (loin, leg)	7–8 minutes per 450 g (1 lb)	As for boned roasting joints of beef above. *Stand* for 1 hour.

Type	Approximate time on LOW setting	Special instructions
On the bone (leg, hand)	7–8 minutes per 450 g (1 lb)	As for beef joints on bone above. *Stand* for 1 hour.
Tenderloin	8–10 minutes per 450 g (1 lb)	*Stand* for 10 minutes.
Chops	8–10 minutes per 450 g (1 lb)	*Separate* during defrosting and arrange 'spoke' fashion. *Stand* for 10 minutes.
Sausages	5–6 minutes per 450 g (1 lb)	*Separate* during defrosting. *Stand* for 5 minutes.
OFFAL		
Liver	8–10 minutes per 450 g (1 lb)	*Separate* during defrosting. *Stand* for 5 minutes.
Kidney	6–9 minutes per 450 g (1 lb)	*Separate* during defrosting. *Stand* for 5 minutes.
BACON		
Rashers	2 minutes per 225 g (8 oz) packet	*Remove* slices from pack and separate after defrosting. *Stand* for 6–8 minutes.

TIME AND SETTINGS FOR COOKING MEAT

Type	Time/Setting	Microwave Cooking Technique(s)
BEEF		
Boned roasting joint (sirloin, topside)	per 450 g (1 lb) Rare: 5–6 minutes on HIGH Medium: 7–8 minutes on HIGH Well: 8–10 minutes on HIGH	*Turn* over joint halfway through cooking time. *Stand* for 15–20 minutes, tented in foil.
On the bone roasting joint (fore rib, back rib)	per 450 g (1 lb) Rare: 5 minutes on HIGH Medium: 6 minutes on HIGH Well: 8 minutes on HIGH	*Shield* bone end with small piece of foil during first half of the cooking time. *Turn* over joint halfway through cooking time. *Stand* as for boned joint.
LAMB/VEAL		
Boned rolled joint (loin, leg, shoulder)	per 450 g (1 lb) Medium: 7–8 minutes on HIGH Well: 8–10 minutes on HIGH	*Turn* over joint halfway through cooking time. *Stand* as for beef.
On the bone (leg and shoulder)	per 450 g (1 lb) Medium: 6–7 minutes on HIGH Well: 8–9 minutes on HIGH	*Shield* as for beef. *Position* fatty side down and turn over halfway through cooking time. *Stands* as for beef.
Crown roast of lamb	9–10 minutes on MEDIUM per 450 g (1 lb) stuffed weight	*Shield* bone tips with foil and overwrap with cling film. *Re-position* partway through cooking time. *Stand* for 20 minutes with foil tenting.

Type	Time/Setting	Microwave Cooking Technique(s)
BACON		
Joints	12–14 minutes on HIGH per 450 g (1 lb)	*Cook* in a pierced roasting bag. *Turn* over joint partway through cooking time. *Stand* for 10 minutes, tented in foil.
Rashers	2 rashers: 2–2½ minutes on HIGH 4 rashers: 4–4½ minutes on HIGH 6 rashers: 5–6 minutes on HIGH 12 minutes on HIGH per 450 g (1 lb)	*Arrange* in a single layer. *Cover* with greaseproof paper to prevent splattering. *Cook* in preheated browning dish if liked. *Remove* paper immediately after cooking to prevent sticking. For large quantities: *Overlap* slices and place on microwave rack. *Re-position* three times during cooking.
OFFAL		
Liver (lamb and calves)	6–8 minutes on HIGH per 450 g (1 lb)	*Cover* with greaseproof paper to prevent splattering.
Kidneys	8 minutes on HIGH per 450 g (1 lb)	*Arrange* in a circle. *Cover* to prevent splattering. *Re-position* during cooking.
Tongue	20 minutes on HIGH per 450 g (1 lb)	*Re-position* during cooking.
Chops	1½ minutes on HIGH, then 1½–2 minutes on MEDIUM	*Cook* in preheated browning dish, or finish off under grill. *Position* with bone ends towards centre.
PORK		
Boned rolled joint (loin, leg)	8–10 minutes on HIGH per 450 g (1 lb)	As for boned rolled lamb above.
On the bone (leg, hand)	8–9 minutes on HIGH per 450 g (1 lb)	As for lamb on the bone above.
Chops	1 chop: 4–4½ minutes on HIGH 2 chops: 5–5½ minutes on HIGH 3 chops: 6–7 minutes on HIGH 4 chops: 6½–8 minutes on HIGH	*Cook* in preheated browning dish, or finish off under grill. *Position* with bone ends towards centre. *Cover* kidney, if attached, with greaseproof paper. *Stand* for 2 minutes for 1 chop, 3–5 minutes for 2–4 chops.
SAUSAGES	2 sausages: 2½ minutes on HIGH 4 sausages: 4 minutes on HIGH	*Pierce* skins. *Cook* in preheated browning dish or finish off under grill. *Turn* occasionally during cooking.

ORIENTAL MEAT BALLS

25 g (1 oz) butter or margarine
1 medium onion, skinned and finely chopped
450 g (1 lb) lean minced beef
25 g (1 oz) fresh brown breadcrumbs
salt and pepper
45 ml (3 tbsp) vegetable oil
1 medium green pepper, seeded and roughly chopped
1 medium red pepper, seeded and roughly chopped
30 ml (2 level tbsp) flour
30 ml (2 level tbsp) soft brown sugar
10 ml (2 tsp) soy sauce
30 ml (2 tbsp) wine vinegar
150 ml (¼ pint) orange juice
150 ml (¼ pint) beef stock
cooked rice, to serve (see page 85)

1 Put the butter into a 1.7 litre (3 pint) ovenproof glass bowl. Microwave on HIGH for 45 seconds until the butter melts, then stir in the onion and cover with cling film, pulling back one corner to vent. Microwave on HIGH for 5–7 minutes until the onion softens.

2 Remove the bowl from the oven and uncover it. Add the minced beef, breadcrumbs and season well with salt and pepper and mix the ingredients well.

3 With damp hands, shape the minced beef mixture into 20 balls, place them on a plate and chill them for at least 30 minutes.

4 Put the oil into a shallow ovenproof dish and microwave on HIGH for 2 minutes until the oil is hot, then add the meat balls and roll them gently in the oil until they are evenly coated. Microwave uncovered on HIGH for 3–4 minutes, turning over the meat balls during the cooking time.

5 Remove the meat balls from the dish and put them aside. Add the peppers to the oil remaining in the dish, cover the top with cling film, pulling back one corner to vent, and microwave on HIGH for 2–3 minutes until the peppers are softened. Add the flour, mix well and microwave on HIGH for 1 minute.

6 Gradually stir in the sugar, soy sauce, vinegar, orange juice and stock. Microwave on HIGH for 3–4 minutes, until boiling and thickened, stirring frequently.

7 Return the meat balls to the dish and gently coat them with the sauce. Cover them with cling film, pulling back one corner to vent. Microwave on HIGH for 2–3 minutes, then reduce the setting and microwave on LOW for 15 minutes. Serve with rice.

Serves 4.

SPICED BEEF CASSEROLE

15 ml (1 tbsp) vegetable oil
1 medium onion, skinned and sliced
3 celery sticks, trimmed, washed and chopped
1 garlic clove, skinned and crushed
50 g (2 oz) lean streaky bacon, rinded and diced
15 ml (1 level tbsp) flour
15 ml (1 level tbsp) mild curry powder
2.5 ml (½ level tsp) ground allspice
450 g (1 lb) lean minced beef
5 ml (1 level tsp) tomato purée
225 g (8 oz) can tomatoes
salt and pepper
½ a cucumber, chopped
25 g (1 oz) cashew nuts (optional)
150 ml (¼ pint) natural yogurt
cooked rice or garlic bread to serve (see pages 85 and 97)

1 Put the oil into a large ovenproof casserole with the celery, garlic and bacon. Cover with cling film, pulling back one corner to vent and microwave on HIGH for 5–7 minutes until the onions and celery are soft. Stir in the flour, curry powder and allspice and microwave on HIGH for 2 minutes, stirring occasionally.

2 Stir in the minced beef, tomato purée, tomatoes, cucumber and nuts, if using.

3 Three-quarters cover with cling film or a casserole lid. Microwave on HIGH for 20–25 minutes, stirring frequently. Gradually stir in the yogurt, re-cover and microwave on HIGH for 2 minutes. Remove from the oven and allow to stand for 5 minutes. Season well with salt and pepper.

4 Serve with rice or garlic bread.

Serves 4.

BEEF OLIVES

25 g (1 oz) butter or margarine
75 g (3 oz) lean streaky bacon, rinded and chopped
1 small onion, skinned and chopped
10 ml (2 tsp) chopped fresh parsley
125 g (4 oz) fresh white breadcrumbs
1.25 ml (¼ level tsp) dried mixed herbs
1 egg, size 6, beaten
½ a lemon
salt and freshly ground pepper
8 thin slices of beef topside, about 700 g (1½ lb) total weight
15 ml (1 level tbsp) prepared English mustard
60 ml (4 level tbsp) seasoned flour
60 ml (4 tbsp) vegetable oil
2 medium onions, skinned and sliced
300 ml (½ pint) beef stock

1 Put the butter into a medium ovenproof glass bowl, and microwave on HIGH for 45 seconds until the butter melts. Add the bacon and onion and mix well. Cover with cling film, pulling back one corner to vent and microwave on HIGH for 4–5 minutes until the onion softens.

2 Remove the bowl from the oven, uncover it and add the parsley, breadcrumbs, herbs, egg, finely grated rind of ½ lemon and 5 ml (1 tsp) of its juice. Season the ingredients very well with salt and pepper and mix them together thoroughly.

3 Trim the meat and flatten it between two sheets of greaseproof paper until it is quite thin. Spread the mustard thinly over each slice of meat, divide the stuffing evenly among the slices of meat and neatly roll up each slice to enclose the stuffing. Secure the rolls with wooden cocktail sticks or fine string.

4 Toss the beef olives in the seasoned flour, shake off the excess and reserve.

5 Put the oil into a shallow ovenproof casserole and microwave on HIGH for 2 minutes until hot. Add the beef olives, turning them in the oil to coat them evenly and microwave on HIGH for 5–6 minutes, turning the meat frequently until it looks opaque. Remove the meat from the dish and put it aside.

6 Add the onions to the oil remaining in the casserole, cover with cling film, pulling back one corner to vent and microwave on HIGH for 5–7 minutes until the onions are softened. Stir in any excess flour and gradually blend in the stock.

7 Return the beef olives to the casserole and three-quarters cover the dish with cling film. Microwave on HIGH for 8–10 minutes, until boiling, then turn the beef olives in the stock. Reduce the setting and microwave on LOW for about 25–30 minutes until the beef olives are tender.

8 Carefully remove the cocktail sticks or string from each beef olive and adjust the seasoning, cover and leave the meat to stand for 5 minutes before serving.

Serves 4.

COTTAGE PIE WITH ALE

15 ml (1 tbsp) vegetable oil
2 medium onions, skinned and thinly sliced
10 ml (2 level tsp) demerara sugar
1 small garlic clove, skinned and crushed
450 g (1 lb) lean minced beef
30 ml (2 level tbsp) plain flour
300 ml (½ pint) beef stock
150 ml (¼ pint) brown ale
2 bay leaves
salt and pepper
900 g (2 lb) potatoes, peeled and diced evenly
10 ml (2 level tbsp) French mustard
60 ml (4 tbsp) milk
1 egg, size 2, beaten
25 g (1 oz) butter or margarine
chopped fresh parsley, to garnish

1 Put the oil into a 1.7 litre (3 pint) ovenproof glass bowl and microwave on HIGH for 1 minute until hot. Stir in the onions, sugar and garlic and cover the bowl with cling film, pulling back one corner to vent. Microwave on HIGH for 5 minutes until the onions are softened.

2 Uncover the bowl and add the mince, then stir well and microwave on HIGH for 2 minutes, stirring to break up the mince. Stir the flour into the mince, then add the stock, ale and bay leaves. Three-quarters cover with cling film, then microwave on HIGH for 20–25 minutes until cooked.

3 Remove the cooked minced beef from the oven and skim any excess fat from the surface. Season it very well with salt and pepper, cover the meat and put it aside.

4 Put the potatoes into a 2.8 litre (5 pint) ovenproof glass bowl and add 60 ml (4 tbsp) cold water. Three-quarters cover with cling film and microwave on HIGH for 8–10 minutes until the potatoes are cooked, stirring once or twice. Remove them from the oven and allow them to stand for 2–3 minutes.

5 Drain any excess water from the potatoes, then mash them well and beat in the mustard, milk, egg and butter, beating the potatoes until they are smooth and creamy. Season well.

6 Spoon the cooked minced beef into a shallow, ovenproof serving dish, then spoon or pipe the mashed potato over the top of the mince.

7 Microwave, uncovered, on HIGH for 4–5 minutes until the cottage pie is piping hot. Garnish it with chopped parsley. (If preferred, the cottage pie may be browned under a hot grill just before serving.)

Serves 4.

SMOKED HAM IN CREAM SAUCE

45 ml (3 tbsp) white wine vinegar
2 shallots, skinned and finely chopped
6 peppercorns, lightly crushed
6 juniper berries, lightly crushed
30 ml (2 tbsp) vegetable oil
4 slices of smoked or cooked ham, about 1 cm (½ inch) thick
150 ml (¼ pint) dry white wine
150 ml (¼ pint) double cream
salt and pepper
25 g (1 oz) butter or margarine
finely chopped fresh tarragon or parsley, to garnish

1 Put the vinegar into a small ovenproof glass bowl with the shallots, peppercorns and juniper berries. Microwave on HIGH for 3–4 minutes until boiling and reduced by half. Remove the vinegar mixture from the oven and set it aside.

2 Preheat a large browning dish to maximum according to the manufacturer's instructions, adding the oil for the last 30 seconds. (Or, put the oil in a shallow ovenproof dish and microwave on HIGH for 1–2 minutes until hot.)

3 Without removing the dish from the oven, place the slices of ham in the hot oil and microwave for 2 minutes, turning over the ham after 1 minute. Remove the ham from the dish and place it on a warm serving dish, then cover and keep it warm. (If necessary, cook two slices of ham at a time.)

4 Stir in the wine and microwave on HIGH for 5 minutes, until boiling, stirring frequently.

5 Strain the reduced vinegar into the sauce. Stir in the cream and season to taste. Microwave on HIGH for 3–4 minutes until the sauce is very hot but not boiling. Cut the butter into small pieces and stir them quickly into the sauce to give it a glaze.

6 Pour the sauce over the ham and then serve it sprinkled with tarragon or parsley to garnish.

Serves 4.

SPINACH STUFFED SADDLE OF LAMB

25 g (1 oz) butter or margarine
1 medium onion, skinned and chopped
300 g (10.6 oz) packet frozen spinach, thawed (see page 78)
25 g (1 oz) fresh breadcrumbs
finely grated rind and juice of ½ a lemon
salt and pepper
about 1.5 kg (3 lb) saddle of lamb, boned
15 ml (2 level tbsp) redcurrant jelly

1 Place the butter in a small ovenproof bowl and microwave on HIGH for 45 seconds until it has melted. Add the onion and cover with cling film, pulling back one corner to vent, and microwave on HIGH for 5–7 minutes until softened.

2 Drain and discard all the excess liquid from the spinach, then add it to the onion with the breadcrumbs, lemon rind and juice; season to taste and mix together well.

3 Place the meat fat side uppermost on a flat surface and score the fat with a sharp knife. Turn the meat over and spread it with the stuffing. Fold over to enclose the stuffing and sew the edges together with fine string to form a neat and even shape.

4 Weigh the joint and calculate the cooking time at 8 minutes per 450 g (1 lb). Place the joint in a roasting bag, securing the end with string or an elastic band, and place it on a roasting rack. Microwave on HIGH for half the cooking time. Remove from the oven and remove the meat from the roasting bag.

5 Place the redcurrant jelly in a small ovenproof bowl and heat for 30 seconds or until melted, then brush it over the lamb. Return the meat to the oven, uncovered, and cook for the remaining time. Leave to stand for 10–15 minutes. To serve, remove the string and carve into thick slices.

Serves 6.

LAMB BURGERS

450 g (1 lb) lean minced lamb
1 large onion, skinned and finely grated
5 ml (1 level tsp) salt
1.25 (¼ level tsp) cayenne pepper
30 ml (2 tbsp) vegetable oil
plain or toasted hamburger buns, to serve
tomato ketchup, to serve (see page 111)

1 Mix the lamb and onion together and season with salt and cayenne pepper.

2 Divide the lamb mixture into four and shape each piece into a neat pattie about 2.5 cm (1 inch) thick.

3 Preheat a large browning dish to maximum according to the manufacturer's instructions, adding the oil for the last 30 seconds. (Or put the oil into a large shallow ovenproof dish and microwave on HIGH for 1–2 minutes until the oil is hot.)

4 Without removing the dish from the oven, press 2 lamb burgers flat on to the hot surface and microwave on HIGH for 2–3 minutes. Turn the burgers over and re-position them and microwave on HIGH for 2–3 minutes until cooked. Repeat with the remaining burgers.

5 Serve the lamb burgers in plain or toasted hamburger buns, with tomato ketchup.

Makes 4.

MINTED LAMB MEAT BALLS

225 g (8 oz) crisp green cabbage, roughly chopped
1 medium onion, skinned and quartered
450 g (1 lb) lean minced lamb
2.5 ml (½ level tsp) ground allspice
salt and pepper
397 g (14 oz) can tomato juice
1 bay leaf
10 ml (2 tsp) chopped fresh mint or 2.5 ml
   (½ level tsp) dried
15 ml (1 tbsp) chopped fresh parsley
cooked rice or noodles, to serve (see page 85)

1 Put the cabbage and onions in a food processor or
blender and mix until finely chopped. Transfer to
an ovenproof glass bowl, cover the top with cling
film, pulling back one corner to vent, and
microwave on HIGH for 2–3 minutes until the
vegetables are softened. Leave for 5 minutes to
cool.

2 Add the lamb and allspice and season with salt
and pepper. Beat together well.

3 Using wet hands, shape the lamb mixture into 16
small balls and place them in a single layer in a
shallow ovenproof dish. Microwave them
uncovered for 5 minutes, carefully turning and
re-positioning the meat balls after 3 minutes.

4 Mix the tomato juice with the bay leaf, mint and
parsley and pour this over the meat balls. Three-
quarters cover the dish with cling film and
microwave on HIGH for 5–6 minutes until the
sauce is boiling and the meat balls are cooked.
Allow them to stand for 5 minutes. Skim off any fat
and serve with rice or noodles.

Serves 4.

LAMB AND APRICOT KEBABS

700 g (1½ lb) lamb fillet or boned leg of lamb
60 ml (4 tbsp) olive oil
juice of 1 lemon
1 garlic clove, skinned and crushed
pinch of salt
5 ml (1 level tsp) ground cumin
5 ml (1 level tsp) ground coriander
5 ml (1 level tsp) ground cinnamon
2 large onions, skinned and quartered
75 g (3 oz) apricots, diced
8 bay leaves
cooked rice, to serve (see page 85)

1 Cut the lamb into 2.5 cm (1 inch) thick slices if
using fillet, or cubes, if using leg.

2 Put the olive oil, lemon juice, garlic, salt, cumin,
coriander and cinnamon into a large glass bowl and
whisk the ingredients together well. Stir in the
lamb, cover and leave it to marinate at room
temperature for at least 4 hours.

3 Put the onion quarters and the apricots into an
ovenproof glass bowl, add 150 ml (¼ pint) water,
cover and microwave on HIGH for 3 minutes.
Drain them well, cover and set them aside until
lamb is ready for cooking.

4 Put alternate pieces of lamb, apricot, onion
quarters and bay leaves on to eight wooden kebab
skewers.

5 Arrange the kebabs in a double layer on a
roasting rack in a shallow ovenproof dish and spoon
over any remaining marinade. Microwave on
HIGH for 8 minutes, then re-position them so that
the inside skewers are moved to the outside of the
dish. Microwave on HIGH for 10 minutes,
re-positioning the kebabs twice during this cooking
period. Allow them to stand for 5 minutes.

6 Serve with rice. The juices left in the bottom of
the cooking dish may be reheated and served
separately with the kebabs.

Serves 4.

PORK FILLET WITH CIDER AND CORIANDER

450 g (1 lb) pork fillet (tenderloin)
30 ml (1 tbsp) vegetable oil
1 small green pepper, seeded and sliced into rings
1 medium onion, skinned and chopped
15 ml (1 level tbsp) ground coriander
15 ml (1 level tbsp) flour
150 ml (¼ pint) dry cider
150 ml (¼ pint) chicken stock
salt and pepper

1 Trim the pork fillet of all fat and membrane. Cut it into 0.5 cm (¼ inch) thick pieces, place between two sheets of greaseproof paper and flatten with a mallet until thin.

2 Put the oil in a shallow ovenproof dish or casserole and microwave on HIGH for about 1 minute. Stir in the pepper and onion, cover with cling film, pulling back one corner to vent, and microwave on HIGH for 5–7 minutes until the vegetables soften.

3 Stir in the flour and coriander and microwave on HIGH for 2 minutes. Gradually stir in the cider and stock and microwave on HIGH for 3–4 minutes, stirring frequently until boiling and thickened. Add the pork, cover with cling film, pulling back one corner to vent, and microwave on HIGH for 5–6 minutes until boiling. Stir. Reduce the setting, microwave on LOW for 7–8 minutes until the pork is tender. Allow it to stand for 5 minutes before serving.

Serves 4.

PORK WITH TOMATO AND BARLEY

4 spare rib pork chops
30 ml (2 tbsp) vegetable oil
2 medium onions, skinned and sliced
397 g (14 oz) can tomatoes
150 ml (¼ pint) chicken stock
50 g (2 oz) pearl barley
1 large garlic clove, skinned and crushed
5 ml (1 level tsp) dried oregano
salt and pepper

1 Trim any excess fat from the chops.

2 Put the oil and onions into an ovenproof casserole dish and mix well. Cover the dish with cling film, pulling back one corner to vent, and microwave on HIGH for 5–7 minutes until the onions are softened.

3 Uncover the dish and lay the chops on top of the onions. Add the tomatoes, stock, barley, garlic and oregano. Cover with cling film, pulling back one corner to vent. Microwave on HIGH for 10 minutes, or until boiling, then reduce the setting and microwave on LOW for 40 minutes until the chops are tender and the barley is soft.

4 Remove the dish from the oven and leave it to stand for 10–15 minutes. Skim off any excess fat and season well with salt and pepper. Serve with jacket potatoes, if wished.

Serves 4.

SAGE AND BACON-STUFFED PORK

about 1.8 kg (4 lb) loin of pork, boned and rinded
8 streaky bacon rashers, rinded
12 fresh sage leaves
2 garlic cloves, skinned and cut into slivers
salt and pepper
fresh sage, to garnish

1 Place the pork, fat side uppermost, on a flat surface and remove most of the fat. Score the remaining fat with a sharp knife.

2 Turn over the meat and lay half of the bacon, the sage and the garlic over the flesh. Season well with salt and pepper. Roll up and secure with string. Lay the remaining bacon on top of the joint.

3 Weigh the joint and calculate the cooking time at 8 minutes per 450 g (1 lb). Place the joint in a roasting bag, securing the end with string and place on a roasting rack, bacon side down. Microwave on HIGH for half of the calculated cooking time, then turn over and cook for the remaining time. Leave to stand for 10–15 minutes. Garnish with fresh sage and serve cut into slices.

Serves 6–8.

PORK CHOPS IN CIDER

2 garlic cloves, skinned and crushed
4 pork chops, trimmed of excess fat
30 ml (2 tbsp) vegetable oil
15 ml (1 level tbsp) plain flour
150 ml (¼ pint) cider
1 fresh rosemary sprig
15 ml (1 tbsp) double cream
salt and pepper

1 Spread the garlic all over the pork chops.

2 Preheat a large browning dish to maximum according to the manufacturer's instructions, adding the oil during the last 30 seconds. (Or, put the oil into a shallow ovenproof dish and microwave on HIGH for 1 minute until hot.)

3 Without removing the dish from the oven, place the chops in the oil and microwave, uncovered, on HIGH for 6–8 minutes, turning them over and re-positioning after 3 minutes. Remove the chops from the dish and set them aside.

4 Stir the flour into the oil remaining in the cooking dish, microwave on HIGH for 1 minute, then gradually stir in the cider.

5 Microwave on HIGH for 3–4 minutes until boiling, stirring frequently. Stir in 30 ml (2 tbsp) water.

6 Return the chops to the dish and add the rosemary, spooning the sauce over the chops. Cover the dish with cling film, pulling back one corner to vent, and microwave on HIGH for about 2 minutes until the sauce returns to the boil. Reduce the setting and microwave on LOW for 15–20 minutes until the chops are tender.

7 Pour the cream over the chops and season well with salt and pepper. Allow them to stand for 5 minutes before serving.

Serves 4.

PORK AND APPLE HOT-POT

4 loin pork chops, each about 2.5 cm (1 inch) thick
50 g (2 oz) butter or margarine
225 g (8 oz) cooking apples, peeled, cored and thickly sliced
1 large onion, skinned and sliced
450 g (1 lb) potatoes, peeled and diced evenly
3 tomatoes, skinned and chopped
about 300 ml (½ pint) chicken stock
salt and pepper

1 Remove the bones and any excess fat from the chops, roll each one into a neat round and secure with a wooden cocktail stick.

2 Put the butter into a deep ovenproof casserole and microwave on HIGH for 45 seconds until the butter melts, then add the apples, onion and potatoes and mix well. Cover the ingredients with cling film, pulling back one corner to vent, and microwave on HIGH for 6–8 minutes until the onion and potatoes begin to soften.

3 Place the chops on top of the vegetables and microwave on HIGH for 2 minutes until the surface of the meat turns opaque.

4 Sprinkle the chopped tomatoes over the chops. Pour chicken stock into the casserole to come halfway up the sides of the vegetables. Cover the casserole with cling film, pulling back one corner to vent. Microwave on HIGH for about 5 minutes until boiling, reduce the setting and microwave on LOW for 40 minutes until the chops are tender, turning them over halfway through cooking.

5 Skim off any excess fat and carefully remove the cocktail sticks from the chops. Season the hot-pot very well with salt and pepper, then cover and leave it to stand for 10 minutes before serving.

Serves 4.

MEAT LOAF

175 g (6 oz) streaky bacon rashers, rinded
25 g (1 oz) butter or margarine
1 small onion, skinned and finely chopped
225 g (8 oz) lamb's liver, washed
225 g (8 oz) lean pork
175 g (6 oz) sausagemeat
15 ml (1 tbsp) brandy
1 egg
salt and pepper
5 ml (1 level tsp) dried mixed herbs
60 ml (4 tbsp) double cream

1 Stretch the bacon with the back of a knife and use it to line a 700 g (1½ lb) ovenproof glass loaf dish.

2 Place the butter in a large ovenproof dish and microwave on HIGH for 30 seconds or until the butter is melted.

3 Add the onion and microwave on HIGH for 5–7 minutes or until soft, stirring occasionally.

4 Coarsely chop the liver and pork and add it to the onion mixture, together with the remaining ingredients. Mix well.

5 Spread the mixture into the loaf dish being careful not to disturb the bacon. Cover with greaseproof paper.

6 Place the dish in another dish containing enough cold water to come half way up the sides of the loaf dish.

7 Microwave on HIGH for 25 minutes or until cooked, removing the greaseproof paper after 15 minutes and giving the dish a quarter turn three times during cooking.

8 When cooked, place a plate on top of the meat loaf and weight it down. Allow it to cool, then chill it overnight in the refrigerator.

9 Serve the meatloaf cut into slices with toast or crackers.

Serves 6.

WIENER SCHNITZEL

6 veal or pork escalopes, cut about 0.5 cm (¼ inch) thick
2 eggs
salt and pepper
75 ml (5 level tbsp) plain flour
175 g (6 oz) dried breadcrumbs
30–60 ml (2–4 tbsp) vegetable oil
lemon wedges and chopped fresh parsley, anchovy fillets and capers (optional), to garnish
green salad, to serve

1 Flatten the escalopes between two sheets of greaseproof paper with a meat mallet until they are about 0.3 cm (⅛ inch) thick. Trim off any excess fat.

2 Beat the eggs with salt and pepper in a shallow dish. Spread the flour on a sheet of greaseproof paper and the breadcrumbs on another.

3 Coat the escalopes in the flour, shaking off the excess, then dip them in the egg and coat them with the breadcrumbs.

4 Preheat a large browning dish to maximum according to the manufacturer's instructions, adding half of the oil for the last 30 seconds.

5 Without removing the dish from the oven, place two escalopes in the hot oil and microwave on HIGH for 1 minute, then turn over the escalopes and microwave on HIGH for ½–1 minute, or until the escalopes are cooked through. Transfer the schnitzels to a hot serving dish, cover and keep them warm.

6 Wipe the browning dish clean with absorbent kitchen paper. Reheat the dish and add the remaining oil for the last 30 seconds. Cook the remaining two escalopes as above and place them on the serving dish.

7 Garnish the escalopes with lemon wedges and parsley, adding anchovy fillets and capers if you wish. Serve the schnitzels with a green salad.

Serves 4.

LIVER WITH ONIONS AND MUSHROOMS

450 g (1 lb) lamb's liver, washed
15 ml (1 level tbsp) flour
50 g (2 oz) butter or margarine
450 g (1 lb) onions, skinned and thinly sliced
4 streaky bacon rashers, rinded and chopped
100 g (4 oz) mushrooms, sliced
salt and pepper
15 ml (1 tbsp) wine vinegar

1 Wash the liver in cold water and cut out any inedible membranes. Pat it dry with kitchen paper.

2 Cut the liver, diagonally, into thick slices and toss them gently in the flour.

3 Preheat a large browning dish to maximum according to the manufacturer's instructions, adding 25 g (1 oz) of the butter for the last minute. (Or, put the butter into a shallow ovenproof dish and microwave on HIGH for 1 minute until butter is bubbling.)

4 Without removing the dish from the oven, place the liver in the hot butter and microwave on HIGH for about 5 minutes, turning the slices over and re-positioning them after 3 minutes. Remove the liver to a hot dish, cover and keep warm.

5 Add the remaining butter to the cooking dish and microwave on HIGH for about 1 minute until bubbling.

6 Stir the onions, bacon and mushrooms into the butter, three-quarters cover the dish with cling film and microwave on HIGH for 5–7 minutes until softened, stirring frequently.

7 Season the onions very well with salt and pepper and stir in the vinegar and liver. Microwave on HIGH for 1 minute and serve hot.

Serves 4.

LIVER AND BEAN CASSEROLE

350 g (12 oz) lamb's liver, washed
25 g (1 oz) plain flour
15 ml (1 tbsp) vegetable oil
1 medium onion, skinned and finely chopped
150 ml (¼ pint) beef stock
75 ml (3 fl oz) milk
30 ml (2 level tbsp) tomato purée
5 ml (1 level tsp) dried mixed herbs
100 g (4 oz) mushrooms, sliced
475 g (17 oz) can red kidney beans, drained
salt and pepper

1 Cut the liver into 1 cm (½ inch) strips and toss in the flour.

2 Heat a browning dish to maximum according to the manufacturer's instructions, adding the oil for the last 30 seconds.

3 Add the liver, any excess flour and the onion and mix well.

4 Microwave on HIGH for 3 minutes, stirring occasionally.

5 Add the stock, milk, purée and herbs and mix well together. Microwave on HIGH for 10 minutes or until boiling, stirring occasionally.

6 Add the mushrooms, kidney beans and seasoning and microwave on HIGH for 5–7 minutes or until the liver is tender. Serve hot with boiled rice (see page 85) or mashed potatoes and a green vegetable.

Serves 4.

SAUSAGE-STUFFED CABBAGE LEAVES

8 large green cabbage leaves, washed
225 g (8 oz) pork sausagemeat
50 g (2 oz) fresh breadcrumbs
salt and pepper
5 ml (1 tsp) chopped fresh sage
100 g (4 oz) mushrooms, sliced
25 g (1 oz) butter or margarine
1 large onion, skinned and chopped
30 ml (1 level tbsp) plain flour
150 ml (¼ pint) chicken stock
150 ml (¼ pint) milk
2 large tomatoes, skinned and sliced

1 Trim the stalk ends of the cabbage leaves and place them on a large ovenproof plate. Cover them with cling film, pulling back one corner to vent, and microwave on HIGH for 2–3 minutes until the leaves soften. Remove them from the oven and immediately plunge them into cold water, then drain well.

2 Mix together the sausagemeat, breadcrumbs, salt and pepper, sage and half the mushrooms. Divide the mixture evenly among the cabbage leaves, placing it at the stalk-end of each leaf. Bring the sides of each leaf to the centre, then roll up the leaf to enclose the sausagemeat in a neat parcel.

3 Put the butter in a shallow ovenproof dish and microwave on HIGH for 45 seconds until the butter melts. Add the onion and remaining mushrooms and mix them well with the butter. Microwave on HIGH for 4–5 minutes until softened.

4 Stir in the flour and microwave on HIGH for 1 minute. Gradually stir in the chicken stock and the milk and microwave on HIGH for about 5 minutes, or until boiling, stirring frequently.

5 Carefully place the stuffed cabbage leaves in the dish, spooning the sauce over them to coat evenly. Cover with cling film, pulling back one corner to vent. Microwave on HIGH for 8 minutes, or until the sausagemeat is cooked, re-positioning the stuffed leaves twice during the cooking time to ensure they cook evenly.

6 Uncover the dish and skim off any excess fat, if necessary. Arrange the tomato slices over the cabbage leaves and then season them well with salt and pepper. Microwave on HIGH for 1–2 minutes, until the tomatoes are hot.

Serves 4.

KIDNEYS IN RED WINE

8 lamb's kidneys
50 g (2 oz) butter or margarine
1 large onion, skinned and chopped
25 g (1 oz) flour
150 ml (¼ pint) red wine
150 ml (¼ pint) beef stock
15 ml (1 level tbsp) tomato purée
bouquet garni
100 g (4 oz) mushrooms, sliced
salt and pepper
chopped fresh parsley, to garnish
cooked rice, to serve (see page 85)

1 Skin the kidneys, cut them in half and remove the cores.

2 Put the butter into a shallow ovenproof dish and microwave on HIGH for 45 seconds until the butter melts. Stir in the onion, cover with cling film and pull back one corner to vent. Microwave on HIGH for 5–7 minutes until the onion softens.

3 Uncover the dish, stir in the flour and microwave on HIGH for 1 minute. Add the kidneys and microwave on HIGH for 3–4 minutes, stirring occasionally. Stir in the wine, stock, tomato purée, bouquet garni and mushrooms, three-quarters cover with cling film and microwave on HIGH for 5 minutes, or until the kidneys are cooked, stirring twice during the cooking time. Uncover and microwave on HIGH for 1 minute.

4 Remove the bouquet garni from the dish and season the kidneys well with salt and pepper. Sprinkle them with chopped parsley and serve them with rice.

Serves 4.

Stuffed trout – served with cucumber sauce is a delicious meal for a summer dinner. Accompany with new potatoes and French beans.
Recipe on page 73.

KIDNEY AND CELERY SAUTE

450 g (1 lb) lamb's kidneys
2 celery sticks, washed and trimmed
15 ml (1 tbsp) vegetable oil
25 g (1 oz) butter or margarine
30 ml (2 tbsp) brandy (optional)
150 ml (¼ pint) beef stock
1 garlic clove, skinned and crushed
salt and pepper
chopped fresh parsley, to garnish

1 Remove the skin from each kidney, cut them in half and snip out the cores, then halve the kidneys again. Slice the celery into 2.5 cm (1 inch) diagonal pieces.

2 Preheat a large browning dish to maximum according to the manufacturer's instructions, adding the oil and butter for the last 30 seconds. (Or put the oil and butter into a shallow ovenproof dish and microwave on HIGH for 1 minute until the butter is bubbling.)

3 Without removing the dish from the oven, place the kidney pieces in the hot oil, turning them quickly so that they are well coated. Microwave on HIGH for 2–4 minutes until cooked. Remove the kidney pieces from the dish and keep them warm.

4 Add the sliced celery to the cooking dish, cover the top with cling film, pulling back one corner to vent, and microwave on HIGH for 3–4 minutes, stirring occasionally, until the celery has softened.

5 Add the kidneys to the celery and stir in the brandy, if using, then microwave on HIGH for 1 minute. Remove the dish from the oven and set the brandy alight, then, when the flame subsides, stir in the stock, garlic, salt and pepper. Microwave on HIGH for 4–5 minutes until boiling, stirring once during the cooking time. Garnish with parsley.

Serves 4.

Ceylon Prawn curry – Prawns in curry sauce is a delicious dish to serve for lunch or dinner. Serve with rice and mixed fruit chutney.
Recipe on page 72.

SPICY MEAT BALLS

45 ml (3 tbsp) vegetable oil
1 medium onion, skinned and finely chopped
2.5 ml (½ level tsp) ground cumin
2.5 ml (½ level tsp) ground coriander
2.5 ml (½ level tsp) ground ginger
2.5 ml (½ level tsp) ground cinnamon
1 garlic clove, skinned and crushed
1 small chilli, finely chopped
50 g (2 oz) fresh brown breadcrumbs
450 g (1 lb) lean pork, minced
1 egg, beaten
salt and pepper
2.5 ml (½ level tsp) ground turmeric
2.5 ml (½ level tsp) cayenne pepper
150 ml (¼ pint) natural yogurt
5 ml (1 level tsp) garam masala

1 Place 15 ml (1 tbsp) of the vegetable oil and the onion in a large shallow ovenproof dish and microwave on HIGH for 5–7 minutes or until soft, stirring occasionally.

2 Stir in the cumin, coriander, ginger, cinnamon, garlic and chilli. Microwave on HIGH for 2 minutes, stirring frequently.

3 Add the breadcrumbs, pork, egg and seasoning, mix together, and shape into 16 small balls.

4 Heat a browning dish to maximum according to the manufacturer's instructions, adding the remaining oil for the last 30 seconds.

5 Add the meat balls to the hot oil and microwave on HIGH for 5 minutes. Re-position the meatballs and microwave for 5 minutes or until cooked.

6 Remove the meat balls with a slotted spoon and arrange them on a heated serving dish.

7 Stir the turmeric and cayenne pepper into the oil remaining in the browning dish and microwave on HIGH for 2 minutes, stirring occasionally.

8 Stir in the yogurt and seasoning and microwave on MEDIUM for 2 minutes to heat through.

9 Pour over the meat balls, sprinkle with the garam masala and serve with boiled rice (see page 85).

Serves 4.

FISH

Fish is one of the best foods to cook in a microwave oven as the cooking time is so brief that the fish retains its juices, texture and shape and – a big advantage – the smell, which can pervade the whole house, is eliminated. Take care not to overcook fish or it will dry out; remember, it continues to cook after the oven is switched off. It is better to undercook it and put it back for a few more seconds if necessary.

When cooking whole fish, first slash the skin in one or two places to prevent it splitting. Arrange the fish so that thin parts are in the centre of the oven and thicker parts are to the outside where they will receive more microwave energy. When cooking more than one fish, overlap the thin parts to prevent them from cooking too quickly and keep them separate with small pieces of cling film or greaseproof paper. This will prevent them sticking together. When cooking more than two large fish,

use an oblong ovenproof dish and move the outside fish to the middle halfway through the cooking time. Large pieces of fish should always be cooked in a single layer, although fillets may be rolled up. Always cover fish with cling film before cooking it to prevent it drying out, and pierce the cling film so that steam can escape.

Shellfish are even more critical when it comes to cooking times as overcooking will cause them to toughen. Where appropriate they can be cooked in their shells.

Canned fish just needs to be drained and then reheated in a suitable container.

Fish which is coated in breadcrumbs (eg, fish fingers) cooks quickly and should be left uncovered so that the coating does not become soggy and lose its crisp texture.

Boil-in-the-bag fish should have the bag pierced before cooking to let steam out.

TIME AND SETTINGS FOR COOKING FISH IN THE MICROWAVE

Type	Time/Setting	Microwave Cooking Technique(s)
Whole round fish (whiting, mullet, trout, carp, bream, small haddock)	3 minutes on HIGH per 450 g (1lb)	*Slash* skin to prevent bursting. *Turn* over fish partway through cooking time. *Shield* tail with small pieces of smooth foil. *Re-position* fish if cooking more than 2.
Whole flat fish (plaice, sole)	3 minutes on HIGH	*Slash* skin. *Turn* dish partway through cooking time. *Shield* tail as for round fish.
Cutlets, steaks, fillets	4 minutes on HIGH per 450 g (1 lb)	*Position* thicker parts towards the outside, overlapping thin ends and separating with cling film. *Turn* over fillets and quarter-turn dish 3 times during cooking.
Smoked fish	4 minutes on HIGH per 450 g (1 lb)	Follow techniques for type of fish above.

DEFROSTING FISH AND SHELLFISH

Separate fish cutlets, fillets or steaks as soon as possible during defrosting. Like poultry, it is best to finish defrosting whole fish in cold water to prevent drying out of the surface. Arrange scallops and prawns in a circle and cover with absorbent kitchen paper to help absorb liquid; remove pieces from the oven as soon as defrosted.

Type	Approximate time on LOW setting	Special instructions
White fish fillets or cutlets, eg cod, coley, haddock, halibut, or whole plaice or sole	3–4 minutes per 450 g (1 lb) plus 2–3 minutes	*Stand* for 5 minutes after each 2–3 minutes.
Oily fish, eg whole and gutted mackerel, herring, trout	2–3 minutes per 225 g (8 oz) plus 3–4 minutes	*Stand* for 5 minutes between defrosts and for 5 minutes afterwards.
Kipper fillets	2–3 minutes per 225 g (8 oz)	As for oily fish above.
Lobster tails, crab claws, etc	3–4 minutes per 225 g (8 oz) plus 2–3 minutes	As for oily fish above.
Crabmeat	2–3 minutes per 450 g (1 lb) block plus 2–3 minutes	As for oily fish above.
Prawns, shrimps, scampi	2½ minutes per 100 g (4 oz) 3–4 minutes per 225 g (8 oz)	*Pierce* plastic bag if necessary. *Stand* for 2 minutes. *Separate* with a fork after 2 minutes. *Stand* for 2 minutes, then plunge into cold water and drain.

COD WITH TOMATOES AND PEPPERS

700 g (1½ lb) cod or haddock fillet, skinned
2 medium onions, skinned and chopped
1 green pepper, seeded and chopped
45 ml (3 tbsp) vegetable oil
30 ml (2 level tbsp) flour
150 ml (¼ pint) fish or chicken stock
5 ml (1 level tsp) tomato purée
397 g (14 oz) can tomatoes
1 bay leaf
1 garlic clove, skinned and crushed
salt and pepper
30 ml (2 tbsp) chopped fresh parsley

1 Cut the fish into 2.5 cm (1 inch) cubes and then set it aside.

2 Place the onion, pepper and vegetable oil in a large ovenproof casserole and mix well. Cover with cling film, pulling back one corner to vent, and microwave on HIGH for 5–7 minutes until softened.

3 Stir in the flour and microwave on HIGH for 1 minute. Gradually stir in the stock, tomato purée and tomatoes and microwave on HIGH for 2–3 minutes until boiling and thickened, stirring every minute.

4 Add the bay leaf, garlic and fish, three-quarters cover with cling film and microwave on HIGH for 8–9 minutes until the fish is coooked, stirring occasionally.

5 Season well with salt and pepper and stir in the parsley. Serve hot.

Serves 4.

COD STEAKS WITH ALMONDS

50 g (2 oz) flaked almonds
6 cod steaks, about 1 cm (½ inch) thick
50 g (2 oz) butter or margarine
salt and pepper
15 ml (1 tbsp) lemon juice
fish or chicken stock
1 medium onion, skinned and chopped
15 ml (1 level tbsp) flour
300 ml (10 fl oz) soured cream

1 Spread the flaked almonds evenly over a flat ovenproof plate. Microwave the nuts on HIGH for 4–5 minutes stirring occasionally, until lightly browned. Set aside.

2 Place the cod steaks in a shallow ovenproof dish with the thickest parts to the outside of the dish. Dot the fish with 25 g (1 oz) of the butter and season well with salt, pepper and lemon juice.

3 Cover the dish loosely with cling film or greaseproof paper and microwave on HIGH for 4 minutes per 450 g (1 lb). Turn over the steaks and re-position them once during cooking.

4 Drain the cooking juices from the cod steaks into a measuring jug and make them up to 300 ml (½ pint) with stock.

5 Place the cod steaks on a large ovenproof serving dish, cover and set aside.

6 Put the remaining 25 g (1 oz) butter in an ovenproof bowl and microwave on HIGH for 30 seconds until the butter melts. Stir in the onion. Cover with cling film, pulling back one corner to vent, and microwave on HIGH for 5–7 minutes until the onion softens.

7 Stir the flour into the onion and microwave on HIGH for 30 seconds. Gradually stir in the stock. Microwave on HIGH for 45 seconds and whisk well. Microwave on HIGH for 1½–2 minutes until the sauce boils, whisking every 30 seconds.

8 Stir the soured cream into the sauce and season well with salt and pepper. Microwave on HIGH for 2–3 minutes until hot but not boiling, stirring every 30 seconds.

9 Stir the almonds into the sauce and pour evenly over the cod steaks. Microwave on HIGH for 2–3 minutes to heat through.

Serves 6.

COD AND CUCUMBER MORNAY

4 large cod cutlets
salt and pepper
10 ml (2 tsp) chopped fresh parsley
150 ml (¼ pint) dry cider
15 g (½ oz) butter or margarine
15 g (½ oz) flour
½ a cucumber, peeled, cut in half lengthways, seeded and sliced
150 ml (¼ pint) milk
100 g (4 oz) Cheddar cheese, grated
slices of lemon and sprigs of watercress, to garnish

1 Place the cod cutlets in a shallow ovenproof serving dish or casserole, season with salt and pepper, add the parsley and pour the cider over them. Cover the dish with cling film, pulling back one corner to vent, and microwave on HIGH for 8–10 minutes until the fish is almost cooked. Remove it from the oven, cover and leave to stand.

2 Put the butter into an ovenproof glass bowl and microwave on HIGH for 45 seconds or until melted. Stir in the flour and microwave on HIGH for 1 minute. Gradually stir in the milk and microwave on HIGH for 2–3 minutes until boiling and thickened, whisking every minute. Stir in the cucumber, three-quarters cover with cling film and microwave on HIGH for 5–6 minutes until the cucumber is softened, stirring once or twice.

3 Season with salt and pepper and pour the cucumber and milk over the cod cutlets. Sprinkle with the cheese. Microwave on HIGH for 5–6 minutes until the cheese melts. Garnish with lemon slices and watercress. If wished this dish may be browned, after cooking, under a hot grill.

Serves 4.

FISH PIE

700 g (1½ lb) cod fillet, even thickness
75 g (3 oz) butter or margarine
about 300 ml (½ pint) milk
salt and pepper
700 g (1½ lb) potatoes, peeled and sliced
1 egg, beaten
25 g (1 oz) flour
3 eggs, hard-boiled and sliced
50 g (2 oz) shelled prawns, (optional)
chopped fresh parsley, to garnish

1 Place the cod in a shallow ovenproof dish, dot with 25 g (1 oz) of the butter, add 150 ml (¼ pint) of the milk and season well with salt and pepper. Cover with cling film, pulling back one corner to vent, and microwave on HIGH for 5–6 minutes until the cod is white and flakes easily, turning the dish two or three times during cooking. Stand for 5 minutes.

2 Strain the juices from the cod into a measuring jug and make up to 300 ml (½ pint) with milk. Remove all the bones and skin from the cod, then flake the flesh. Set aside.

3 Put the potatoes in a large ovenproof bowl with 90 ml (6 tbsp) water and three-quarters cover it with cling film. Microwave on HIGH for 12–15 minutes until the potatoes are cooked, stirring two or three times during cooking.

4 Drain any excess water from the potatoes. Mash and cream the potatoes with 25 g (1 oz) butter and the beaten egg.

5 Put the remaining 25 g (1 oz) butter in an ovenproof bowl and microwave on HIGH for 30 seconds until the butter melts, stir in the flour and microwave on HIGH for 30 seconds. Gradually stir in the measured milk. Microwave on HIGH for 45 seconds, then whisk well. Microwave on HIGH for 1¾–2 minutes until boiling, whisking every 30 seconds. Season well with salt and pepper.

6 Fold the flaked cod, prawns and eggs into the sauce, then pour into a large ovenproof serving dish, or pie dish.

7 Spoon or pipe the cooked potatoes over the fish mixture. Microwave on HIGH for 5–6 minutes until the pie is well heated through. Sprinkle with chopped parsley and serve immediately.

Serves 4.

HERRINGS WITH MUSTARD SAUCE

90 g (3½ oz) butter or margarine
45 ml (3 level tbsp) flour
450 ml (¾ pint) milk
30 ml (2 level tbsp) mustard powder
20 ml (4 tsp) malt vinegar
salt and pepper
30 ml (2 tbsp) single cream
4 large herrings, cleaned and heads removed
watercress, to garnish

1 Put the butter into a medium ovenproof glass bowl and microwave on HIGH for 45 seconds until the butter melts. Stir in the flour and microwave on HIGH for 1 minute. Gradually stir in the milk. Microwave on HIGH for 45 seconds and whisk well. Microwave on HIGH for 2–3 minutes until the sauce boils, whisking every minute.

2 Blend the mustard powder with the vinegar and stir into the sauce. Season with salt and pepper and stir in the cream. Cover the surface of the sauce closely with cling film to prevent a skin forming and set aside.

3 Scrape the scales from the herrings with the back of a knife, and remove the fins. Slash the skin three times on each side of each herring, season well with salt and pepper. Beat the remaining butter in a bowl until soft and spread on both sides of the fish.

4 Place the herrings in a shallow ovenproof serving dish. Loosely cover with cling film and microwave on HIGH for 2–3 minutes. Turn over the herrings and re-position. Loosely cover with cling film and microwave on HIGH for a further 2–3 minutes until the flesh flakes easily. Remove the herrings from the oven and keep warm.

5 Reheat the mustard sauce on HIGH for 2–3 minutes, whisking every minute. Pour some of the sauce over the fish and serve the rest separately. Garnish with watercress.

Serves 4.

SAVOURY HADDOCK CRUMBLE

700 g (1½ lb) haddock fillet
about 300 ml (½ pint) milk
salt and pepper
75 g (3 oz) butter or margarine
1 medium onion, skinned and chopped
2 eggs, hard-boiled and chopped
25 g (1 oz) capers, drained (optional)
15 g (½ oz) plain flour
75 g (3 oz) plain wheatmeal flour
25 g (1 oz) rolled oats
chopped fresh parsley, to garnish

1 Put the haddock, milk, salt and pepper into a shallow ovenproof dish, Cover with cling film, pulling back one corner to vent, and microwave on HIGH for 6–8 minutes until the haddock is cooked and flakes easily.

2 Strain the milk from the haddock into a measuring jug and make up to 300 ml (½ pint) with a little more milk, if necessary.

3 Skin and flake the haddock, removing the bones.

4 Put 25 g (1 oz) of the butter into a shallow ovenproof serving dish and microwave on HIGH for 30 seconds until the butter melts. Add the onion and cover with cling film, pulling back one corner to vent, and microwave on HIGH for 4–7 minutes until the onion softens.

5 Stir in the plain flour and microwave on HIGH for 1 minute. Gradually stir in the measured milk then microwave on HIGH for 45 seconds and then whisk well. Microwave on HIGH for 2–3 minutes until boiling, whisking every minute. Season well with salt and pepper. Stir in the fish, egg and capers, if using.

6 To make the crumble topping, rub the remaining 50 g (2 oz) butter into the wheatmeal flour until the mixture resembles breadcrumbs. Stir in the oats and season with salt and pepper. Sprinkle the topping evenly over the fish mixture. Microwave on HIGH for 9–10 minutes. Leave to stand for 5 minutes before serving, garnished with parsley.

Note: The crumble may be browned under a hot grill after cooking if wished.

Serves 4.

BAKED MACKEREL

50 g (2 oz) butter or margarine
1 small onion, skinned and finely chopped
1 eating apple, peeled and coarsely grated
50 g (2 oz) Cheddar cheese, grated
25 g (1 oz) fresh breadcrumbs
finely grated rind of ½ an orange
salt and pepper
4 mackerel, cleaned and heads removed
60 ml (4 tbsp) fresh orange juice
orange wedges and chopped fresh parsley, to garnish

1 Put 25 g (1 oz) of the butter into an ovenproof bowl and microwave on HIGH for 30 seconds until the butter melts. Add the onion. Cover with cling film, pulling back one corner to vent, and microwave on HIGH for 3–4 minutes until the onion softens.

2 Stir the apple, cheese, breadcrumbs and orange rind into the softened onion and season very well with salt and pepper.

3 Fill each fish with the apple stuffing and secure the opening with wooden cocktail sticks. Slash the skin three times on each side.

4 Put the remaining butter into a large shallow ovenproof dish large enough to take the fish in a single layer. Microwave on HIGH for 1 minute until melted. Stir in the orange juice.

5 Place the fish in the dish side by side and cover with greaseproof paper. Microwave on HIGH for 3 minutes, turn over the mackerel and re-position them so that the outside fish are in the middle. Re-cover and microwave on HIGH for 3–4 minutes until the fish are cooked and the flesh flakes easily. Remove the cocktail sticks.

6 Garnish the mackerel with orange wedges and parsley and serve immediately.

Serves 4.

SEAFOOD PANCAKES

40 g (1½ oz) butter or margarine
225 g (8 oz) piece of monkfish
100 g (4 oz) wheatmeal flour
salt and pepper
1 egg
568 ml (1 pint) milk
vegetable oil, for frying
25 g (1 oz) plain flour
5 ml (1 tsp) lemon juice
5 ml (1 level tsp) tomato purée
100 g (4 oz) Cheddar cheese, grated
100 g (4 oz) peeled shrimps
50 g (2 oz) shelled cockles
15 ml (1 tbsp) chopped fresh parsley

1 Beat 15 g (½ oz) of the butter in a bowl until soft, then spread it over the monkfish. Place in a shallow ovenproof dish and cover with cling film, pulling back one corner to vent. Microwave on HIGH for 5–6 minutes until the fish is just cooked and flakes easily, turning over after 3 minutes. Cover and leave the fish to stand while making the pancakes.

2 Put the wheatmeal flour and a good pinch of salt into a mixing bowl. Make a well in the centre of the flour and break in the egg. Gradually add 150 ml (¼ pint) of the milk, vigorously beating in the flour until a thick smooth batter is formed. Pour in a further 150 ml (¼ pint) milk and beat again.

3 Heat a little oil in a frying-pan and when it is very hot pour in a small amount of batter. Tip the pan quickly so that the batter runs over the bottom of the pan to coat it thinly. Cook over a high heat for about 1 minute until the underside is golden brown, then turn the pancake over and cook the other side until golden brown. Remove it from the pan and keep it warm. Make seven more pancakes in the same way.

4 Remove any skin from the monkfish, flake the flesh and remove the bones. Put fish aside.

5 Put the remaining 25 g (1 oz) butter into an ovenproof bowl and microwave on HIGH for 30 seconds until the butter melts. Stir in the flour and microwave on HIGH for 1 minute. Gradually stir in the remaining milk. Microwave on HIGH for 45 seconds, then whisk well. Microwave on HIGH for 1½–2 minutes until the sauce boils, whisking every 30 seconds.

6 Stir the lemon juice, tomato purée and half of the cheese into the hot sauce. Fold in the flaked monkfish, the shrimps and cockles. Season well with salt and pepper.

7 Divide the fish mixture evenly among the pancakes and neatly roll them up to enclose the filling. Place the pancakes side by side in a buttered shallow ovenproof dish. Sprinkle with the remaining cheese and the parsley. Cover with cling film, pulling back one corner to vent, and microwave on HIGH for 5–6 minutes until the pancakes are well heated through. Serve hot with a green salad.

Serves 4.

POACHED PLAICE IN CIDER

50 g (1 oz) butter or margarine
175 g (6 oz) carrots, peeled and finely sliced
3 celery sticks, washed, trimmed and finely sliced
15 g (½ oz) flour
200 ml (7 fl oz) dry cider
juice of ½ a lemon
8 plaice fillets, skinned
175 g (6 oz) button mushrooms, sliced
226 g (8 oz) can tomatoes, drained
salt and pepper

1 Put the butter into a shallow ovenproof dish and microwave on HIGH for 45 seconds until the butter melts. Add the carrots and celery and mix well. Three-quarters cover with cling film and microwave on HIGH for 8–10 minutes until the carrots soften. Stir in the flour and microwave on HIGH for 1 minute. Gradually stir in the cider and lemon juice.

2 Roll up the plaice fillets with the skin side inside, then place them on top of the vegetables. Scatter the mushrooms and tomatoes over the fish and season well with salt and pepper.

3 Cover the dish with cling film, pulling back one corner to vent, and microwave on HIGH for 10–11 minutes until the fish and vegetables are cooked. Turn the dish two or three times during cooking. Uncover and microwave on HIGH for 2 minutes. Serve hot.

Serves 4.

CEYLON PRAWN CURRY

50 g (2 oz) butter or margarine
1 large onion, skinned and finely chopped
1 garlic clove, skinned and crushed
15 ml (1 level tbsp) flour
10 ml (2 level tsp) turmeric
2.5 ml (½ level tsp) ground cloves
5 ml (1 level tsp) ground cinnamon
5 ml (1 level tsp) salt
5 ml (1 level tsp) sugar
50 g (2 oz) creamed coconut
450 ml (¾ pint) chicken stock
450 g (1 lb) peeled prawns or 12 Dublin Bay prawns,
  peeled
5 ml (1 tsp) lemon juice
cooked rice (see page 85) and chutney, to serve
fresh coriander sprigs, to garnish

1 Put the butter into a shallow ovenproof dish and microwave on HIGH for 1 minute until the butter melts; stir in the onion and garlic. Cover with cling film, pulling back one corner to vent, and microwave on HIGH for 5–7 minutes until the onion softens.

2 Stir the flour, spices, salt and sugar into the onion. Microwave on HIGH for 2 minutes. Stir in the creamed coconut and stock. Microwave on HIGH for 6–8 minutes until boiling, stirring frequently.

3 Add the prawns and lemon juice to the sauce and adjust the seasoning. Microwave on HIGH for 1–2 minutes until the prawns are heated through. Garnish with the coriander and serve with rice and chutney.

Serves 4.

LEMON-POACHED SALMON STEAKS

100 g (4 oz) butter or margarine
30 ml (2 tbsp) finely chopped fresh mixed herbs
salt and pepper
200 ml (7½ fl oz) dry white wine
1 small carrot, peeled and very finely sliced
1 celery stick, washed, trimmed and very finely sliced
1 small onion, skinned and very finely sliced
1 bay leaf
6 white peppercorns, crushed
4 parsley sprigs
5 ml (1 level tsp) salt
thinly peeled rind and strained juice of 1 lemon
4–6 2.5 cm (1 inch) thick salmon steaks

1 To make the herb butter, cream the butter until soft. If it is very hard, microwave on HIGH for 10 seconds until soft. Stir in the herbs, salt and pepper and beat together well. Shape the butter into a roll and wrap it in greaseproof paper or kitchen foil. Leave it in the refrigerator to harden while cooking the fish.

2 Put the wine, vegetables, bay leaf, peppercorns, parsley, salt, lemon rind and juice into a deep ovenproof casserole and add 450 ml (¾ pint) water. Cover with the lid and microwave on HIGH for 8 minutes or until the liquid is boiling.

3 Uncover the casserole and gently lower in the salmon steaks. Replace the lid and microwave on HIGH for 3 minutes or until the liquid starts to bubble.

4 Microwave on HIGH for a further 2–3 minutes until the fish is tender. Give the dish a half turn halfway through cooking.

5 Replace the lid after testing the fish and leave it to stand for 5 minutes. While the fish is standing, cut the butter into slices about 0.5 cm (¼ inch) thick. Remove the fish carefully with a slotted spoon. Serve hot with the herb butter.

Serves 4–6.

STUFFED TROUT

25 g (1 oz) butter or margarine
1 medium onion, skinned and finely chopped
75 g (3 oz) fresh breadcrumbs
30 ml (2 tbsp) chopped fresh parsley
finely grated rind and juice of 1 lemon
salt and pepper
4 whole trout, about 225 g (8 oz) each, cleaned and
  eyes removed
lemon wedges and chopped fresh parsley or tarragon, to
  garnish
cucumber sauce, to serve (see page 109)

1 Put the butter into a medium ovenproof glass
bowl and microwave on HIGH for 1 minute until
the butter melts. Stir in the onion. Cover with
cling film, pulling back one corner to vent, and
microwave on HIGH for 5–7 minutes until the
onion softens. Stir in the breadcrumbs, parsley,
lemon rind and juice and the salt and pepper and
mix together well.

2 Fill each trout with the stuffing, then slash the
skin twice on each side. Place the trout side by side
in a large ovenproof dish.

3 Cover with cling film, pulling back one corner to
vent, and microwave on HIGH for 8–10 minutes,
turning the trout over and re-positioning them
halfway through cooking. Stand for 5 minutes
before serving. Garnish with lemon wedges and
parsley or tarragon and serve with cucumber sauce.

Serves 4.

TUNA AND CHEESE QUICHE

25 g (1 oz) butter or margarine
1 onion, skinned and chopped
2 eggs
300 ml (½ pint) milk
salt and pepper
100 g (4 oz) Cheddar cheese, grated
198 g (7 oz) can tuna, drained and flaked
20.5 cm (8 inch) pre-baked pastry flan case

1 Put the butter into an ovenproof glass bowl and
microwave on HIGH for 30 seconds until the butter
melts. Add the onion and cover with cling film,
pulling back one corner to vent. Microwave on
HIGH for 5–7 minutes until the onion softens,
then leave to cool.

2 Add the eggs, the milk, and the salt and pepper
to the onion and lightly whisk together. Stir in the
cheese.

3 Place the flan case on a flat ovenproof plate.
Spread the tuna in the bottom of the flan case and
pour in the cheese and milk mixture. Microwave on
MEDIUM for 23–24 minutes until the filling is just
set. Leave to stand for 5 minutes before serving.

Serves 4–6.

WHOLE FISH COOKED CHINESE STYLE

*2 whole fish such as mullet, carp, bream, cleaned, about
   450 g (1 lb) total*
2.5 cm (1 inch) piece of root ginger, peeled
2 spring onions, trimmed
1 carrot, peeled
50 g (2 oz) ham
50 g (2 oz) mushrooms, thinly sliced
45 ml (3 tbsp) dry sherry
30 ml (2 tbsp) soy sauce
5 ml (1 level tsp) sugar
salt and pepper
spring onion tassels, to garnish

1 Slash the fish skin 3 times on each side to allow
for even cooking and to prevent bursting.

2 Place the fish in a shallow ovenproof dish.

3 Thinly shred the ginger, onions, carrot and ham
and sprinkle these over the fish, together with the
mushrooms.

4 Mix the remaining ingredients together and
spoon them over the fish.

5 Cover with cling film and microwave on HIGH
for 3–4 minutes per 450 g (1 lb) or until the fish is
tender, turning the fish over halfway through
cooking.

6 Serve garnished with spring onion tassles.

Serves 2.

FISH KEBABS

450 g (1 lb) cod fillet
1 small green pepper, seeded
1 small onion, skinned and finely chopped
30 ml (2 tbsp) olive or vegetable oil
10 ml (2 tsp) lemon juice
*15 ml (1 tbsp) chopped fresh mixed herbs or 5 ml
   (1 level tsp) dried*
salt and pepper
8 button mushrooms
8 bay leaves
8 cherry tomatoes

1 Cut the fish and pepper into 2.5 cm (1 inch)
cubes.

2 Mix together the onion, olive oil, lemon juice,
herbs and seasoning in a large ovenproof glass bowl.
Add the fish, pepper, mushrooms and bay leaves
and leave to marinate for 1 hour.

3 Remove the fish from the marinade with a slotted
spoon and set aside.

4 Cover the bowl of marinated vegetables with
cling film and microwave on HIGH for 3 minutes,
stirring once.

5 Thread the cod, pepper, tomatoes, mushrooms
and bay leaves on to eight wooden skewers and
brush with the marinade.

6 Arrange the kebabs in a double layer on a
roasting rack and microwave on HIGH for
4 minutes, then re-position them, brush with any
remaining marinade and microwave on HIGH for
5–6 minutes or until the fish is tender.

7 Serve hot with boiled rice (see page 85) or a
green salad.

Serves 4.

VEGETABLES

Cooking vegetables, whether fresh or frozen, is one of the areas where a microwave oven excels. Because little or no water is used, the vegetables retain texture, shape, colour and, above all, nutrients. In addition, they cook in a quarter to a third of the time they take to cook conventionally. The following rules apply:

Don't salt vegetables before cooking them. Because salt attracts moisture it distorts the pattern of the microwaves and causes uneven cooking and toughening of the vegetables. Add salt when cooking is completed, stirring it well into the vegetables so it dissolves.

Vegetables which are to be cooked in their skins should have them pierced or slit to prevent pressure building up and the flesh bursting out. This applies to potatoes, aubergines, peppers and tomatoes.

To skin vegetables such as tomatoes or aubergines, microwave them briefly on High, then plunge them into cold water after which the skins should rub off easily.

Vegetables which contain a lot of water can be cooked in just the water they are washed in, with no extra added. These include mushrooms, courgettes, marrow, spinach and sliced tomatoes.

Small vegetables like peas, broad beans and corn kernels need the addition of a little water before cooking.

Root vegetables cook best if cut into even-sized pieces and covered with water. The cooking time will depend on the age and density of the vegetables.

Vegetables with tough stems, such as broccoli and calabrese, should be arranged in a circle in a little water with the stems towards the outside edge where more microwaves will reach them.

Frozen vegetables are always cooked on High and need no water added to them unless the quantity is very large.

Canned vegetables should be drained, rinsed and then heated through until they are hot.

Dried vegetables should be soaked in water before they are cooked. See also Pulses on page 85.

Fresh vegetables to be frozen can be blanched in the microwave in small quantities of about 450 g (1 lb) at a time. Place them in 45–60 ml (4–5 tbsp) water and microwave them on High for 2 minutes. Stir them and then microwave them for a further 1–2 minutes until all the pieces are hot. Drain the vegetables, plunge them into ice-cold water, re-drain them and then pack and freeze.

Fresh herbs can be dried in the microwave, then crushed and stored in dark airtight jars. Place them on absorbent kitchen paper and microwave them on High until the herbs are brittle and dry. Finally, crush them between two pieces of absorbent kitchen paper.

FRESH VEGETABLES

Vegetables need very little water added when microwaved. In this way they retain their colour, flavour and nutrients more than they would if cooked conventionally. They can be cooked in boil-in-the-bags, plastic containers and polythene bags – make sure there is a space for steam to escape.

Prepare vegetables in the normal way. It is most important that food is cut to an even size and stems are of the same length. Vegetables with skins, such as aubergines, need to be pierced before microwaving to prevent bursting. Either season vegetables with salt after cooking or add salt to the water beforehand. Salt distorts the microwave patterns and dries the vegetables.

Vegetable	Quantity	Approximate time on HIGH setting	Microwave Cooking Technique(s)
ARTICHOKE, GLOBE	1 2 3	5–6 MINUTES 7–8 MINUTES 11–12 MINUTES	*Place* upright in covered dish.
ASPARAGUS	350 g (12 oz)	5–7 minutes	*Place* stalks towards the outside of the dish. *Re-position* during cooking.
AUBERGINE	450 g (1 lb) sliced	8–10 minutes	*Stir* or *shake* after 4 minutes.
BEANS, BROAD	450 g (1 lb)	6–8 minutes	*Stir* or *shake* after 3 minutes and test after 5 minutes.
BEANS, GREEN	450 g (1 lb)	12–16 minutes	*Stir* or *shake* during the cooking period. Time will vary with age and size.
BEETROOT, WHOLE	4 medium	14–16 minutes	*Pierce* skin with a fork. *Re-position* during cooking.
BROCCOLI	450 g (1 lb)	10–12 minutes	*Re-position* during cooking. *Place* stalks towards the outside of the dish.
BRUSSELS SPROUTS	225 g (8 oz) 450 g (1 lb)	4–6 minutes 7–10 minutes	*Stir* or *shake* during cooking.
CABBAGE	450 g (1 lb) quartered or shredded	9–12 minutes	*Stir* or *shake* during cooking.
CARROTS	450 g (1 lb)	10–12 minutes	*Stir* or *shake* during cooking.
CAULIFLOWER	whole 225 g (8 oz) florets 450 g (1 lb) florets	12–16 minutes 7–8 minutes 10–12 minutes	*Stir* or *shake* during cooking.
CELERY	450 g (1 lb) sliced	7–10 minutes	*Stir* or *shake* during cooking.
CORN-ON-THE-COB	2	6–8 minutes	*Wrap* individually in greased greaseproof paper. *Do not* add water. *Turn* over after 3 minutes.

Vegetable	Quantity	Approximate time on HIGH setting	Microwave Cooking Technique(s)
COURGETTES	450 g (1 lb) sliced	8–12 minutes	*Do not* add more than 30 ml (2 tbsp) water. *Stir* or *shake* gently twice during cooking. *Stand* for 2 minutes before draining.
FENNEL	450 g (1 lb) sliced	9–10 minutes	*Stir* and *shake* during cooking.
LEEKS	450 g (1 lb) sliced	10–12 minutes	*Stir* or *shake* during cooking.
MUSHROOMS	225 g (8 oz)	2–3 minutes	*Do not* add water. Add 25 g (1 oz) butter and a squeeze of lemon juice. *Stir* or *shake* gently during cooking.
ONIONS	225 g (8 oz) sliced	4–6 minutes	*Stir* or *shake* sliced onions. *Add only* 60 ml (4 tbsp) water to whole onions. *Re-position* whole onions during cooking.
	175 g (6 oz) whole	10–12 minutes	
PARSNIPS	450 g (1 lb)	10–16 minutes	*Place* thinner parts towards the centre. *Add* a knob of butter and 15 ml (1 tbsp) lemon juice with 150 ml (¼ pint) water. *Turn* dish during cooking and *re-position*.
PEAS	450 g (1 lb)	9–11 minutes	*Stir* or *shake* during cooking.
POTATOES Baked jacket	1 × 175 g (6 oz) potato	4 minutes	*Wash* and prick the skin with a fork. *Place* on absorbent kitchen paper or napkin. When cooking more than 2 at a time, arrange in a circle. *Turn* over halfway through cooking.
	2 × 175 g (6 oz) potatoes	6–8 minutes	
	4 × 175 g (6 oz) potatoes	12–14 minutes	
Boiled (old)	450 g (1 lb)	7–10 minutes	*Stir* or *shake* during cooking.
Boiled (new)	450 g (1 lb)	6–8 minutes	*Do not* overcook or new potatoes become spongy.
Sweet	450 g (1 lb)	5 minutes	*Wash* and prick the skin with a fork. *Place* on absorbent kitchen paper. *Turn* over halfway through cooking time.
SPINACH	450 g (1 lb)	6–7 minutes	*Do not* add water. Best cooked in roasting bag, sealed with non-metal fastening. *Turn* dish during cooking.
SWEDE/TURNIP	450 g (1 lb) diced	10–15 minutes	*Stir* or *shake* during cooking.

FROZEN VEGETABLES COOKING CHART

Frozen vegetables may be cooked straight from the freezer. Many may be cooked in their original plastic packaging or pouch, as long as it is first slit and then placed on a plate or in a dish.

Vegetable	Quantity	Approximate time on HIGH setting	Further instructions
ASPARAGUS	275 g (10 oz)	7–9 minutes	*Separate* and *re-arrange* after 3 minutes.
BEANS, BROAD	225 g (8 oz)	7–8 minutes	*Stir* or *shake* during cooking period.
BEANS, GREEN CUT	225 g (8 oz)	6–8 minutes	*Stir* or *shake* during cooking period.
BROCCOLI	275 g (10 oz)	7–9 minutes	*Re-arrange* spears after 3 minutes.
BRUSSELS SPROUTS	225 g (8 oz)	6–8 minutes	*Stir* or *shake* during cooking period.
CAULIFLOWER FLORETS	275 g (10 oz)	7–9 minutes	*Stir* or *shake* during cooking period.
CARROTS	225 g (8 oz)	6–7 minutes	*Stir* or *shake* during cooking period.
CORN-ON-THE-COB	1 2	3–4 minutes 6–7 minutes	*Do not* add water. Dot with butter, wrap in greaseproof paper.
MIXED VEGETABLES	225 g (8 oz)	5–6 minutes	*Stir* or *shake* during cooking period.
PEAS	225 g (8 oz)	5–6 minutes	*Stir* or *shake* during cooking period.
PEAS AND CARROTS	225 g (8 oz)	7–8 minutes	*Stir* or *shake* during cooking period.
SPINACH, LEAF OR CHOPPED	275 g (10 oz)	7–9 minutes	*Do not* add water. Stir or shake during cooking period.
SWEDE/TURNIP, DICED	225 g (8 oz)	6–7 minutes	*Stir* or *shake* during cooking period. Mash with butter after standing time.
SWEETCORN	225 g (8 oz)	4–6 minutes	*Stir* or *shake* during cooking period.

BROCCOLI WITH LEMON

700 g (1½ lb) broccoli, trimmed
15 ml (1 tbsp) vegetable oil
1 small onion, skinned and finely chopped
1 garlic clove, skinned and crushed (optional)
grated rind and juice of 1 lemon
150 ml (¼ pint) chicken stock
1.25 ml (¼ level tsp) salt

1 Cut off the flower heads from the broccoli and divide them into small florets. Thinly peel the stalks and cut them into 0.5 cm (¼ inch) slices.

2 Put the oil, onion and garlic into a casserole and mix them well. Cover with a lid or with cling film, pulling back one corner to vent. Microwave on HIGH for 4–5 minutes until the onion softens.

3 Place the prepared broccoli on top of the onion and sprinkle it with the lemon rind and juice. Pour in the stock.

4 Cover with a lid or cling film, pulling back one corner to vent. Microwave on HIGH for 7–8 minutes until the broccoli is tender, carefully turning and re-positioning the sprigs halfway through the cooking time. Season with salt.

Serves 4 as an accompaniment.

RUNNER BEANS PROVENCALE

30 ml (2 tbsp) olive oil
1 medium onion, skinned and chopped
1 garlic clove, skinned and crushed
397 g (14 oz) can tomatoes, drained
700 g (1½ lb) runner or French beans
15 ml (1 tbsp) chopped fresh basil
salt and pepper
chopped fresh parsley or basil, to garnish

1 Put the oil into an ovenproof glass bowl with the onion and garlic and mix well. Cover with cling film, pulling back one corner to vent. Microwave on HIGH for 5–6 minutes until softened.

2 Stir the tomatoes, salt and pepper into the onions. Microwave on HIGH for 5–6 minutes until the tomatoes are very soft and have formed a thick purée, stirring frequently. Set them aside.

3 Top and tail the beans and cut them into 5 cm (2 inch) lengths.

4 Put the beans into an ovenproof glass bowl with 90 ml (6 tbsp) water. Three-quarters cover the beans with cling film and microwave on HIGH for 12–14 minutes until the beans are tender but still crisp, stirring them frequently. Allow them to stand for 3 minutes and then drain them well.

5 Stir the tomato purée, and basil into the beans and then spoon them into an ovenproof serving dish. Cover and microwave on HIGH for 1 minute. Season with salt and pepper. Serve the beans sprinkled with parsley or basil.

Serves 4–6.

CABBAGE WITH CARAWAY SEEDS

700 g (1½ lb) white cabbage
5 ml (1 level tsp) caraway seeds
2.5 ml (½ level tsp) grated nutmeg
1 onion, skinned and chopped
30 ml (2 tbsp) chicken stock
15 g (½ oz) butter or margarine
salt and pepper

1 Cut the cabbage into quarters and wash it well. Remove the thick stem and shred the cabbage finely, using a sharp knife.

2 Place the cabbage in a large ovenproof serving dish with the caraway seeds, nutmeg, onion and stock. Three-quarters cover with cling film.

3 Microwave on HIGH for 10–12 minutes, stirring frequently, until the cabbage is cooked. Add the butter and the salt and pepper, toss well and serve.

Serves 6 as an accompaniment.

CREAMED CARROTS AND PARSNIPS

900 g (2 lb) carrots, peeled and sliced
450 g (1 lb) parsnips, peeled and cut into quarters, core removed, and sliced
50 g (2 oz) butter or margarine
salt and pepper
pinch of ground nutmeg
chopped fresh parsley, to garnish

1 Put the carrots and the parsnips into a large ovenproof bowl and add 150 ml (¼ pint) water. Three-quarters cover with cling film and microwave on HIGH for 20–30 minutes until the vegetables are cooked, stirring frequently. Allow them to stand for 3 minutes, then drain very well.

2 Mash the carrots and the parsnips with a potato masher, beat in the butter and season well with nutmeg.

3 Spoon the mixture into an ovenproof serving dish and loosely cover with cling film. Microwave on HIGH for 2–3 minutes to heat through the mixture. Season with salt and pepper. Garnish it with parsley and serve.

Serves 4–6 as an accompaniment.

79

BRAISED CELERY

2 small heads celery, washed, trimmed and halved
50 g (2 oz) butter or margarine
1 large carrot, peeled and chopped
1 medium onion, skinned and chopped
bouquet garni
600 ml (1 pint) chicken stock
45 ml (3 level tbsp) flour
salt and pepper

1 Remove the outer stalks and trim the tops off the celery heads. Reserve a few leaves as a garnish.

2 Put 25 g (1 oz) of the butter into a shallow ovenproof dish large enough to take the celery heads in a single layer. Microwave the butter on HIGH for 45 seconds until it is melted.

3 Stir the carrot and onion into the melted butter and cover them with cling film, pulling back one corner to vent. Microwave on HIGH for 7 minutes until the vegetables are softened.

4 Place the celery heads on top of the carrot and onion, add the bouquet garni and pour in the chicken stock. Cover with cling film, pulling back one corner to vent. Microwave on HIGH for 10–15 minutes until the celery heads are tender, turning them and changing their position twice during the cooking time.

5 Carefully remove the celery and keep it warm in a heated serving dish. Reserve 450 ml (¾ pint). Discard the bouquet garni.

6 Put the remaining butter in an ovenproof glass bowl and microwave on HIGH for 1 minute until it is melted; stir in the flour and microwave on HIGH for 1 minute. Gradually stir in the stock and microwave on HIGH for 45 seconds, then whisk well. Microwave on HIGH for 2–3 minutes until the sauce boils and thickens, whisking every 30 seconds.

7 Pour the sauce over the celery and microwave on HIGH for 1 minute to heat it through. Season with salt and pepper. Serve the celery garnished with the reserved celery leaves.

Serves 4 as an accompaniment.

COURGETTES WITH TOMATOES AND CHEESE

15 g (½ oz) butter or margarine
1 shallot or small onion, skinned and chopped
1 garlic clove, skinned and crushed
450 g (1 lb) courgettes, trimmed and thickly sliced
450 g (1 lb) tomatoes, skinned, halved and quartered
100 g (4 oz) Cheddar cheese, grated
salt and pepper

1 Put the butter into a medium ovenproof glass bowl and microwave on HIGH for 30 seconds. Stir in the onions and garlic and microwave on HIGH for 2 minutes.

2 Mix the courgettes into the onions and three-quarters cover the vegetables with cling film. Microwave on HIGH for about 5 minutes until the courgettes are almost cooked, stirring two or three times during the cooking time.

3 Stir the sliced tomatoes into the courgettes and continue to microwave on HIGH for 2 minutes until the tomatoes are soft.

4 Arrange the vegetables and cheese in layers in a shallow ovenproof serving dish, ending with a layer of cheese. Season with salt and pepper. Microwave on HIGH for 3–4 minutes until the cheese melts. Brown the top under a hot grill and serve immediately.

Serves 4 as an accompaniment or 2 as a main dish.

Spiced wheat peppers – Yellow and green peppers, stuffed with bulger wheat and onions makes a nutritious main course. Serve with cucumber and yogurt sauce.
Recipe on page 83.

LEEK AND BACON HOT-POT

450 g (1 lb) potatoes, washed, peeled and thickly sliced
700 g (1½ lb) leeks, trimmed, washed and thinly sliced
90 g (3½ oz) butter or margarine
175 g (6 oz) lean streaky bacon, rinded
40 g (1½ oz) flour
450 ml (¾ pint) milk
175 g (6 oz) Cheddar cheese, grated
5 ml (1 level tsp) mustard powder
salt and pepper
25 g (1 oz) fresh breadcrumbs

1 Put the potatoes into a large ovenproof glass bowl with 60 ml (4 tbsp) water, three-quarters cover with cling film and microwave on HIGH for 8–10 minutes until the potatoes are tender but not mushy; drain them well.

2 Put the sliced leeks into a large ovenproof bowl and dot them with 25 g (1 oz) of the butter. Three-quarters cover with cling film and microwave on HIGH for 8–10 minutes until the leeks are soft, stirring them once or twice during the cooking time.

3 Place the bacon on a large plate lined with absorbent kitchen paper, and cover it with a layer of paper. Microwave on HIGH for 4–4½ minutes until the bacon is cooked.

4 Place the remaining butter in an ovenproof glass bowl and microwave on HIGH for 45 seconds until it is melted, stir in the flour and microwave on HIGH for 45 seconds.

5 Gradually stir the milk into the roux, then microwave on HIGH for 1 minute. Whisk well and then microwave on HIGH for 2–3 minutes until the sauce is boiling and thickened, whisking every 30 seconds.

6 Add 100 g (4 oz) of the cheese and the mustard to the sauce and stir until the cheese melts. Season the sauce with salt and pepper, then stir in the leeks.

7 Arrange the potatoes in the bottom of a buttered, shallow ovenproof dish and arrange the bacon on the top. Pour the leek mixture over the bacon.

8 Mix the remaining cheese with the breadcrumbs and sprinkle this over the top of the hot-pot. Microwave on HIGH for 5–6 minutes to heat through the hot-pot, then brown the top under a hot grill.

Serves 4 as a main dish.

MUSHROOMS BORDELAISE

30 ml (2 tbsp) olive oil
450 g (1 lb) large mushrooms, wiped and sliced
15 ml (1 tbsp) lemon juice
30 ml (2 tbsp) finely chopped shallots
1–2 garlic cloves, skinned and crushed
30 ml (2 tbsp) finely chopped fresh parsley
salt and pepper

1 Put the oil in a large, shallow ovenproof dish and microwave on HIGH for 1–2 minutes until hot.

2 Stir the mushrooms into the hot oil. Mix the lemon juice, shallots, garlic and parsley together and sprinkle them over the mushrooms.

3 Cover the dish with a lid or with cling film, pulling back one corner to vent. Microwave on HIGH for about 5 minutes until the mushrooms are tender, shaking the dish occasionally. Season with salt and pepper.

Serves 4 as an accompaniment.

Vegetable and chick-pea casserole – An economical and delicious meal which need only be served with a light accompaniment.
Recipe on page 87.

NEW POTATOES WITH SPICED HOLLANDAISE SAUCE

25 g (1 oz) flaked almonds
900 g (2 lb) new potatoes
20 ml (4 level tbsp) turmeric
2 egg yolks
1 garlic clove, skinned and crushed
175 g (6 oz) unsalted butter
30 ml (2 tbsp) natural yogurt
salt and pepper

1 Spread the almonds over a large, flat ovenproof plate. Microwave on HIGH for 7–8 minutes, stirring occasionally, or until the almonds are lightly browned, then put them aside.

2 Wash the potatoes well but do not peel them, cut them in half if they are large and put them into a large ovenproof bowl. Mix together 15 ml (3 level tsp) turmeric and 150 ml (¼ pint) water and pour this over the potatoes.

3 Three-quarters cover the potatoes with cling film and microwave on HIGH for 8–10 minutes until the potatoes are tender, turning frequently.

4 Leave the potatoes to stand for 5 minutes, then drain them well. Put the potatoes into a hot serving dish, cover and keep them warm.

5 Mix together the egg yolks and garlic in a medium ovenproof glass bowl. Cut the butter into small pieces into a small ovenproof bowl and microwave on HIGH for 1 minute until it is melted, then whisk it thoroughly into the egg yolks. Microwave on HIGH for 45 seconds until the sauce is just thick enough to coat the back of a spoon, whisking every 15 seconds – do not overcook or the sauce will curdle.

6 Whisk the yogurt and the remaining turmeric into the sauce and microwave on HIGH for 15 seconds. Season with salt and pepper.

7 Pour the hollandaise sauce over the potatoes, sprinkle with the toasted almonds and serve immediately.

Serves 4–6.

POTATO AND PARSLEY BAKE

25 g (1 oz) butter or margarine
1 medium onion, skinned and thinly sliced
1 garlic clove, skinned and crushed (optional)
142 ml (5 fl oz) soured cream
45 ml (3 tbsp) chopped fresh parsley
700 g (1½ lb) potatoes, peeled and very thinly sliced
salt and pepper
50 g (2 oz) Cheddar cheese, grated
chopped fresh parsley, to garnish

1 Place the butter in a shallow heatproof dish and microwave on HIGH for 30 seconds or until melted.

2 Stir in the onion and garlic and microwave on HIGH for 5–7 minutes or until the onion is soft.

3 Add the cream, parsley and potatoes and mix together well so that the potato slices are coated with the cream mixture.

4 Three-quarters cover with cling film and microwave on HIGH for 15–17 minutes or until the potatoes are tender. Give the dish a quarter turn three times during cooking. Season well with salt and pepper.

5 Sprinkle with the grated cheese and microwave on HIGH for 1–2 minutes or until the cheese is melted. Brown under a preheated grill if desired. Serve hot, garnished with chopped parsley.

Serves 4.

SPICED WHEAT PEPPERS

75 g (3 oz) bulgar wheat
2 green peppers, about 150 g (5 oz) each
1 yellow or red pepper, about 150 g (5 oz)
50 g (2 oz) butter or margarine
2 medium onions, skinned and chopped
5 ml (1 level tsp) chilli powder
5 ml (1 level tsp) ground cumin
300 ml (½ pint) natural yogurt
75 g (3 oz) cucumber, peeled, halved, seeded and finely chopped
chopped fresh parsley, to garnish
salt and pepper

1 Place the wheat in a mixing bowl and cover it with cold water. Cover the bowl and leave the wheat to stand for 1 hour.

2 Cut each pepper in half vertically and remove the seeds. Finely chop one of the green peppers.

3 Alternating the colours, place the halved peppers side by side in a shallow ovenproof dish and add 60 ml (4 tbsp) water. Cover the dish with a lid or with cling film, pulling back one corner to vent. Microwave on HIGH for 6 minutes, re-positioning the peppers three times during the cooking time. Remove them from the oven and leave them to stand while preparing the filling.

4 Put the butter into an ovenproof dish and microwave on HIGH for 1 minute until the butter melts, then stir in the chopped pepper, onions, chilli powder and cumin.

5 Cover the dish with cling film, pulling back one corner to vent, and microwave on HIGH for 5–7 minutes until the onions and pepper are soft. Add the well-drained bulgar wheat and microwave on HIGH for 1 minute, stirring twice during the cooking time.

6 Drain almost all of the water from the peppers. Fill the peppers with the wheat filling and cover with a lid or with cling film, pulling back one corner to vent. Microwave on HIGH for 10 minutes, giving the dish a quarter turn three times during the cooking time.

7 Put the yogurt and cucumber into a small ovenproof glass bowl and microwave on HIGH for 30–45 seconds until they are hot but not boiling, then season well with salt and pepper.

8 Sprinkle the peppers with the chopped parsley, season well with salt and pepper, and serve them with the cucumber and yogurt sauce served separately.

Serves 4 as an accompaniment or 2 as a main dish.

OKRA WITH COCONUT

450 g (1 lb) okra, washed and well dried
30 ml (2 tbsp) light sesame or vegetable oil
2.5 ml (½ level tsp) white mustard seeds
2 medium onions, skinned and thickly sliced
5 ml (1 level tsp) paprika
2.5 ml (½ level tsp) ground coriander
1.25 ml (¼ level tsp) cayenne pepper
50 g (2 oz) fresh grated, or desiccated, coconut
15 ml (1 tbsp) finely chopped fresh coriander leaves
salt and pepper

1 Cut off the stalk ends from the okra and wash and dry it thoroughly.

2 Put the oil into a shallow casserole dish and microwave on HIGH for 2 minutes until hot, then sprinkle in the sesame seeds and stir in the onions. Cover with a lid or with cling film, pulling back one corner to vent.

3 Microwave the onions on HIGH for 5–7 minutes until they are softened, then stir in the okra and the remaining ingredients.

4 Cover the dish with a lid or three-quarters cover with cling film. Microwave on HIGH for 6–8 minutes until the okra is tender but still retains its shape, stirring two or three times during the cooking time. Season with salt and pepper. Serve hot.

Serves 4.

STUFFED COURGETTES

6 medium courgettes, about 700 g (1½ lb)
50 g (2 oz) butter or margarine
1 medium onion, skinned and chopped
198 g (7 oz) can sweetcorn, drained
100 g (4 oz) peeled prawns
30 ml (2 level tbsp) plain flour
300 ml (½ pint) milk
150 g (5 oz) Cheddar cheese, grated
salt and pepper

1 Place the courgettes in a polythene bag with 60 ml (4 tbsp) water. Loosely seal the bag with an elastic band. Microwave on HIGH for 6 minutes.

2 Drain the courgettes, then cut a thin slice off the top of each lengthways and scoop out the flesh, leaving a 0.5 cm (¼ inch) rim around the edge. Roughly chop the flesh including the top slices. Arrange the courgette shells in a large shallow heatproof dish.

3 Place half of the butter in a large ovenproof glass bowl and microwave on HIGH for 30 seconds or until melted. Add the onion and microwave on HIGH for 5–7 minutes or until soft.

4 Stir in the chopped courgette and microwave on HIGH for 6 minutes or until soft, stirring occasionally. Add the sweetcorn and prawns.

5 Spoon the mixture into the courgette shells spreading any excess over the top.

6 Place the remaining butter in a large ovenproof glass bowl and microwave on HIGH for 30 seconds or until melted. Next, stir in the flour and microwave on HIGH for 1 minute.

7 Gradually whisk in the milk and microwave on HIGH for 3 minutes or until thickened, whisking occasionally. Stir in three-quarters of the grated cheese.

8 Pour the sauce over the stuffed courgettes and microwave on HIGH for 3 minutes or until heated through. Season well with salt and pepper.

9 Sprinkle with the remaining cheese and microwave on HIGH for 1–2 minutes or until the cheese is melted.

Serves 6.

SPINACH WITH NUTMEG

1.8 kg (4 lb) fresh spinach
50 g (2 oz) butter, cut into cubes
grated nutmeg
30 ml (2 tbsp) double cream
salt and pepper

1 Trim the spinach, removing any coarse stalks. Wash well in several changes of cold water. Drain thoroughly in a colander.

2 Place the butter in a large ovenproof glass bowl and microwave on HIGH for 1 minute or until melted.

3 Coarsely chop the spinach and stir into the hot butter. Season well with grated nutmeg.

4 Cover and microwave on HIGH for 6–7 minutes or until just tender.

5 Stir in the cream and microwave on HIGH for 1 minute or until heated through. Season with salt and pepper and serve hot.

Serves 4.

PASTA, GRAINS AND PULSES

You will save no time cooking pasta and rice in a microwave oven compared to cooking them conventionally but there is the advantage that they will not stick or burn on the base of the pan. This is because they do not come into contact with a heat source. Nonetheless, pasta still needs to have 15 ml (1 tbsp) oil added to each 1.4 L (2½ pints) water to prevent the pieces sticking to each other. Where a microwave is useful for pasta and rice dishes is in reheating and cooking them from frozen, both of which can be done without drying out or loss of texture.

Both pasta and rice need to be cooked in boiling water and it is quicker to boil the water in an electric kettle than in a microwave oven. Use a large container as both pasta and rice treble in volume when they are cooked.

Fresh pasta takes only about 3 minutes in boiling water; dried pasta and rice will take about 10–12 minutes, depending on the quantity being cooked. Allow a standing time of about 10 minutes and, if you are adding a sauce, it is a good idea to use this time to either make or reheat it.

Frozen pasta and rice can be cooked directly from frozen on the High setting unless combined with a sauce which might spoil or curdle, in which case reheat it for a longer time on the Low setting. The time needed is usually as long as when cooking from fresh.

Pulses, too, take just as long to cook in a microwave as conventionally – and longer than in a pressure cooker. They also require soaking overnight before they are cooked. The most useful types for cooking in a microwave are those such as lentils which can be cooked straight from the packet. Otherwise, the microwave can be used to reheat dishes containing pulses which may have been frozen or to prepare dishes from scratch using canned pulses which just require heating through. Never use a HIGH setting for cooked pulses or they will disintegrate.

RICE AND PASTA

Although there are no real time savings in cooking rice and pasta in the microwave, it may be a more foolproof way of cooking as there is no risk of it sticking to the pan. Standing is necessary to complete cooking.

Dried peas and beans are not recommended for microwaving. The skins remain tough and will burst during cooking. Split lentils, however, can be successfully microwaved because they are not completely encased in a skin.

Type and quantity	Time on HIGH setting	Microwave cooking technique(s)
White long grain rice 225 g (8 oz)	10–12 minutes	*Stir* once during cooking. *Stand* for 10 minutes.
Brown rice, 100 g (4 oz)	30 minutes	As for white long grain rice.
Pasta shapes, 225 g (8 oz) dried	7 minutes	*Stir* once during cooking. *Stand* for 5 minutes.
Spaghetti, tagliatelli, 225 g (8 oz) dried	7–8 minutes	*Stand* for 10 minutes.

LENTILS WITH RICE

50 g (2 oz) flaked almonds
50 g (2 oz) butter or margarine
50 g (2 oz) piece of fresh ginger, scraped and finely
  chopped
1 large onion, skinned and finely chopped
2 garlic cloves, skinned and crushed
2.5 ml (½ level tsp) turmeric
2.5 ml (½ level tsp) chilli
5 ml (1 level tsp) cumin seeds
3 large tomatoes, skinned, seeded and chopped
275 g (10 oz) long grain rice
175 g (6 oz) green lentils
salt and pepper
30 ml (2 tbsp) chopped fresh coriander or parsley
750 ml (1¼ pints) boiling chicken stock
3 tomato slices, to garnish
1 coriander sprig, to garnish

1 Place the almonds on a large ovenproof plate or
baking tray and microwave on HIGH for 8–10
minutes, stirring occasionally, until browned.

2 Put the butter into a large casserole dish and
microwave on HIGH for 45 seconds until melted.

3 Add the ginger, onion and garlic. Cover with
cling film and microwave on HIGH for 5–6
minutes until the onion softens. Stir in the spices
and microwave on HIGH for 2 minutes.

4 Add the tomatoes, rice, lentils, salt and pepper to
the spice mixture and stir well to coat. Microwave
on HIGH for 3 minutes, stirring once.

5 Add half of the coriander or parsley and the stock
to the casserole and stir well. Three-quarters cover
with cling film and microwave on HIGH for about
10–12 minutes, or until the rice and lentils are just
tender and most of the stock has been absorbed.
Using a fork, stir once during the cooking time.

6 Stir the rice and the lentils once again and cover
them tightly with a lid. Leave them to stand for
about 5 minutes, during which time all the liquid
should be absorbed.

7 Fluff up the rice with a fork and garnish it with
the tomato slices and coriander. Serve immediately.

Serves 8.

CURRIED CARROTS AND LENTILS

25 g (1 oz) flaked almonds
30 ml (2 tbsp) vegetable oil
1 medium onion, skinned and very finely chopped
225 g (8 oz) carrots, peeled and thinly sliced
1 garlic clove, skinned and crushed
1.25 ml (¼ level tsp) ground cumin
1.25 ml (¼ level tsp) ground coriander
1.25 ml (¼ level tsp) ground cinnamon
175 g (6 oz) red lentils, rinsed and drained
salt and pepper
1 litre (1¾ pints) boiling chicken stock

1 Place the almonds on a large ovenproof plate and
microwave on HIGH for 8–10 minutes, stirring
frequently until brown, then reserve.

2 Put the oil in a large ovenproof glass bowl and
stir in the onion, carrots and garlic. Microwave on
HIGH for 5–6 minutes, or until the vegetables
soften. Stir them occasionally during cooking.

3 Stir in the spices and lentils and then microwave
on HIGH for 3 minutes, stirring occasionally.

4 Add salt and pepper and the boiling stock and
stir well. Microwave on HIGH for 25 minutes or
until the lentils are just tender, stirring occasionally
during cooking. Serve hot, garnished with the
toasted almonds.

Serves 4.

SPINACH AND LENTIL TIMBALE

50 g (2 oz) lentils
25 g (1 oz) butter or margarine
1 medium onion, skinned and finely chopped
900 g (2 lb) fresh spinach, washed, trimmed and
  roughly chopped, or two 226 g (8 oz) packets frozen
  spinach, thawed
150 ml (¼ pint) milk
150 ml (¼ pint) single cream
4 eggs, beaten
50 g (2 oz) Cheddar cheese, grated
25 g (1 oz) fresh breadcrumbs
pinch of grated nutmeg
salt and pepper

1 Grease a 2.3 litre (4 pint) ring mould. Place the
lentils in a large ovenproof bowl with 300 ml
(½ pint) water. Cover with cling film, pulling back
one corner to vent, and microwave on HIGH for
6–8 minutes until the lentils are soft, stirring
occasionally. Leave them to cool for 10 minutes,
then place them in a food processor or blender and
purée them until smooth.

2 Place the butter in a large ovenproof glass bowl
and microwave on HIGH for 45 seconds until
melted. Stir in the onion and spinach, three-
quarters cover with cling film and microwave on
HIGH for 5–7 minutes until the vegetables are soft,
stirring occasionally.

3 Stir in the milk and cream and microwave on
HIGH for 30–45 seconds until warm but not
boiling. Add the eggs, cheese, breadcrumbs and
lentil purée and season well with nutmeg, salt and
pepper.

4 Pour the mixture into the ring mould and
microwave on MEDIUM for 18–20 minutes until
set. Leave to stand for 5 minutes, then turn out on
to a warmed serving plate and serve.

Serves 6.

VEGETABLE AND CHICK-PEA CASSEROLE

4 courgettes, washed, trimmed and cut into 1 cm
  (½ inch) lengths
1 red pepper, seeded and chopped
1 green pepper, seeded and chopped
2 medium onions, skinned and roughly chopped
2 carrots, peeled and thinly sliced
225 g (8 oz) turnips, peeled and thinly sliced
1 small cauliflower, trimmed, washed and cut into
  florets
4 large tomatoes, skinned, seeded and chopped
100 g (4 oz) tenderised dried apricots, cut into quarters
2 garlic cloves, skinned and crushed
425 g (15 oz) can chick-peas, drained
25 g (1 oz) almonds, blanched
5 ml (1 level tsp) turmeric
10 ml (2 level tsp) paprika
2.5 ml (½ level tsp) coriander
salt and pepper
600 ml (1 pint) vegetable stock
chopped fresh coriander or parsley, to garnish

1 Place all of the prepared vegetables, the apricots,
the garlic, chick-peas and almonds in a large
casserole dish and stir in the spices, the salt, pepper
and stock. Cover the dish with a lid or with cling
film, pulling back one corner to vent.

2 Microwave on HIGH for 8–10 minutes until the
vegetables come to the boil, then microwave for a
further 30–40 minutes until the vegetables are well
cooked. Stir two or three times during cooking.
Serve garnished with coriander or parsley.

Serves 6.

RICE WITH BACON AND PEAS

25 g (1 oz) butter or margarine
4 rashers streaky bacon, rinded and chopped
1 large onion, skinned and chopped
200 g (7 oz) long grain rice
350 g (12 oz) frozen peas
225 g (8 oz) mushrooms, wiped and chopped
400 ml (14 fl oz) boiling chicken stock
15 ml (2 tbsp) chopped fresh parsley
salt and pepper
freshly grated Parmesan cheese, to serve

1 Put the butter into a large casserole dish and microwave on HIGH for 30 seconds until the butter melts. Stir in the bacon and onion. Cover the dish with a lid or with cling film, pulling back one corner to vent. Microwave on HIGH for 5–6 minutes until the onion softens.

2 Add the rice to the casserole and microwave on HIGH for 2 minutes, stirring once. Add the peas and the mushrooms and microwave on HIGH for another 2 minutes.

3 Pour the stock into the casserole, add the parsley and season with salt and pepper. Cover and microwave on HIGH for 10–11 minutes until the rice is just tender and most of the liquid is absorbed. Stir once during the cooking time.

4 Remove the casserole from the oven, stir the rice with a fork, then cover it tightly and leave it to stand for 5 minutes, during which time most of the liquid should be absorbed.

5 Serve sprinkled with grated Parmesan cheese.

Serves 6.

NOODLES IN WALNUT SAUCE

100 g (4 oz) walnut pieces
25 g (2 oz) butter, softened
1 garlic clove, skinned and crushed
150 ml (¼ pint) soured cream
salt and pepper
5 ml (1 tsp) vegetable oil
275 g (10 oz) green tagliatelle
grated Parmesan cheese, to serve

1 In a blender or food processor blend together the walnuts, butter, garlic, soured cream and seasoning.

2 Boil 2 litres (3½ pints) water in a kettle and pour it into either a deep casserole dish or a 2.8 litre (5 pint) ovenproof glass bowl. Add 10 ml (2 level tsp) salt and the vegetable oil.

3 Bring the water back to a full rolling boil in the microwave oven set on HIGH. Quickly lower the tagliatelle into the water, three-quarters cover with cling film and microwave on HIGH for 5 minutes until it is partially cooked.

4 Remove the bowl from the oven and leave the tagliatelle to stand, covered, for about 2 minutes until it is cooked and firm to the bite. Drain well.

5 Place the tagliatelle in a large ovenproof serving dish and add the nut mixture. Toss gently until the tagliatelle is well coated. Microwave on HIGH for 1–2 minutes until it is hot. Sprinkle the tagliatelle with Parmesan cheese and serve it with a green salad.

Serves 4.

CANNELLONI

1 quantity of Basic meat sauce, made as instructed on
page 19

750 ml (1¼ pints) milk
1 small onion, skinned and sliced
1 small carrot, peeled and sliced
2 bay leaves
8 peppercorns
1 parsley sprig
50 g (2 oz) breadcrumbs
50 g (2 oz) freshly grated Parmesan cheese
150 ml (¼ pint) strong beef stock
1 egg, beaten
nutmeg
salt and pepper
10 ml (2 tsp) vegetable oil
18 cannelloni tubes
100 g (4 oz) butter
60 g (2½ oz) flour

1 Put the milk into a large ovenproof glass bowl
with the onion, carrot, bay leaves, peppercorns and
parsley. Microwave on HIGH for 4–5 minutes until
the milk comes just to the boil.

2 Remove the milk from the oven, cover and leave
it to infuse for 30–40 minutes.

3 Put the breadcrumbs and 30 ml (2 level tbsp) of
the Parmesan cheese into a small mixing bowl, pour
in the beef stock, stir well and leave the mixture to
stand for 10 minutes.

4 Mix the breadcrumb mixture and egg into the
ragù. Season it well with freshly grated nutmeg, salt
and pepper.

5 Boil 2.3 litres (4 pints) water in a kettle and pour
it into a deep casserole dish or a 2.8 litre (5 pint)
ovenproof glass bowl. Add 10 ml (2 level tsp) salt
and 5 ml (1 tsp) of the oil.

6 Bring the water back to a full rolling boil in the
microwave oven set on HIGH. Quickly lower the
cannelloni tubes into the water, cover and
microwave on HIGH for 5 minutes until they are
partially cooked.

7 Remove the bowl from the oven and cover it
tightly with foil. Leave the cannelloni to stand for
about 3 minutes until it is cooked and is firm to the
bite.

8 Drain the cannelloni well and then lay them on
clean tea-towels to absorb the excess moisture.

9 Strain the milk and discard the vegetables.

10 Put 75 g (3 oz) of the butter into a large
ovenproof glass bowl and microwave on HIGH for
1 minute until the butter melts. Stir in the flour
and microwave on HIGH for 45 seconds.

11 Gradually stir the flavoured milk into the roux
and microwave on HIGH for 1 minute, then whisk
well. Microwave on HIGH for 4–5 minutes until
the sauce is boiling and thickened, stirring with a
whisk every 30 seconds. Season the sauce well with
salt, pepper and freshly grated nutmeg.

12 Fill the cannelloni tubes with the meat sauce
and place them side by side in a large, shallow
buttered ovenproof dish.

13 Pour the sauce over the cannelloni, sprinkle it
with the remaining cheese and dot with the
remaining butter. Microwave on HIGH for
5 minutes until well heated through and the sauce
is bubbling hot. Brown the top under a hot grill and
serve immediately.

Serves 6.

PASTA IN SOURED CREAM SAUCE

salt and pepper
10 ml (2 tsp) vegetable oil
350 g (12 oz) pasta shapes, such as cartwheels, twists
* or bows*
100 g (4 oz) butter or margarine
2 shallots, skinned and chopped
30 ml (2 level tbsp) flour
150 ml (¼ pint) chicken stock
150 ml (¼ pint) dry white wine
150 ml (¼ pint) soured cream or natural yogurt
100 g (4 oz) button mushrooms, quartered
100 g (4 oz) Cheddar cheese, grated
50 g (2 oz) black olives
200 g (7 oz) can tuna, drained
chopped fresh parsley, to garnish

1 Boil 2 litres (3½ pints) water in a kettle and pour into a 2.8 litre (5 pint) ovenproof glass bowl. Add 10 ml (2 level tsp) salt and half of the vegetable oil.

2 Bring the water back to a full rolling boil in the microwave oven set on HIGH. Quickly lower the pasta into the water, stir once and cover with cling film. Microwave on HIGH for 7 minutes.

3 Remove the bowl from the oven, leave the pasta to stand for 5 minutes until it is cooked firm to the bite. Drain well.

4 Put 50 g (2 oz) of the butter into a large ovenproof serving dish and microwave on HIGH for 45 seconds until melted. Stir in the shallots and cover the bowl with cling film, pulling back one corner to vent. Microwave on HIGH for 4–5 minutes until the shallots are soft.

5 Stir the flour into the shallots and microwave on HIGH for 1 minute. Gradually stir in the stock and the wine and microwave on HIGH for 45 seconds, then whisk well. Microwave on HIGH for 2 minutes until the sauce is boiling and has thickened. Continue to microwave further on HIGH for 1 minute.

6 Stir the soured cream and pasta into the sauce and season it well with salt and pepper. Add the mushrooms, cheese, olives and tuna and mix gently together.

7 Cover with cling film and microwave on HIGH for 2 minutes, or until hot.

Serves 4.

MACARONI CHEESE

100 g (4 oz) butter or margarine
225 g (8 oz) short cut macaroni
1 small onion, skinned and finely chopped
½ green pepper, seeded and finely chopped
2.5 ml (½ level tsp) salt
1.25 ml (¼ level tsp) mustard powder
450 ml (¾ pint) boiling water
225 g (8 oz) Cheddar cheese, grated

1 Put the butter into a large casserole dish and microwave on HIGH for 1 minute or until the butter has melted.

2 Add the macaroni, onion and pepper to the butter and stir well. Cover the dish with a lid or three-quarters cover with cling film and microwave on HIGH for 4–5 minutes, stirring once or twice.

3 Add the salt, mustard and water to the macaroni. Re-cover and microwave on HIGH for about 5 minutes until the macaroni is almost cooked, stirring once during the cooking time.

4 Remove the macaroni from the oven and cover it tightly. Leave it to stand for 5 minutes, until the macaroni is completely cooked.

5 Add the grated cheese to the macaroni and stir until the cheese melts. Serve immediately.

Serves 4.

MACARONI AND TUNA BAKE

225 g (8 oz) short cut macaroni
salt and pepper
198 g (7 oz) can tuna, drained and flaked
225 g (8 oz) cottage cheese
75 g (3 oz) Cheddar cheese, grated
225 g (8 oz) courgettes, thinly sliced
397 g (14 oz) can chopped tomatoes with their juice

1 Place the macaroni in a 2.6 litre (4½ pint) ovenproof glass bowl and pour over 1.7 litres (3 pints) boiling water; add salt to taste. Cover with cling film and microwave on HIGH for 7 minutes. Leave to stand, covered.

2 Mix the tuna, cottage cheese and two thirds of the Cheddar together. Season well with salt and pepper.

3 Line the bottom of a heatproof casserole dish with one third of the courgettes. Spread with half of the tuna mixture.

4 Drain the macaroni and spread half on top of the tuna mixture. Repeat the layers, finishing with a layer of courgettes.

5 Pour over the can of tomatoes, spreading the tomatoes evenly over the courgettes.

6 Three-quarters cover with cling film and microwave on HIGH for 12–15 minutes or until the courgettes are tender.

7 Sprinkle with the remaining cheese and microwave on HIGH for 1–2 minutes or until the cheese is melted. Brown under a preheated grill if desired.

Serves 4.

NUT CUTLETS

40 g (1½ oz) butter or margarine
15 g (½ oz) flour
150 ml (¼ pint) milk
1 small onion, skinned and finely chopped
1 garlic clove, skinned and crushed
50 g (2 oz) mushrooms, wiped and chopped
50 g (2 oz) fresh brown breadcrumbs
75 g (3 oz) Cheddar cheese, grated
50 g (2 oz) salted peanuts, finely chopped
50 g (2 oz) shelled brazil nuts, finely chopped
1.25 ml (¼ level tsp) vegetable extract
salt, pepper and lemon juice, to taste
15 ml (1 tbsp) chopped fresh parsley

1 Put 15 g (½ oz) of the butter into an ovenproof glass bowl and microwave on HIGH for 30 seconds until melted. Stir in the flour and microwave on HIGH for 30 seconds.

2 Gradually stir the milk into the roux. Microwave on HIGH for 30 seconds, then whisk well. Microwave for 1 minute on HIGH, or until boiling and thickened, whisking once. Cover the surface of the sauce with cling film to prevent a skin forming. Set aside.

3 Put the remaining butter into an ovenproof dish and microwave on HIGH for 30 seconds until melted; stir in the onion, garlic and mushrooms. Three-quarters cover with cling film and microwave on HIGH for 4–5 minutes until softened, stirring once.

4 Stir the breadcrumbs into the onion and mushrooms, then add them and all the remaining ingredients to the thick sauce, mixing together well.

5 Shape the mixture into a long roll about 18 cm (7 inches) long, then cut the roll into eight even-sized pieces. Shape each piece into a neat round.

6 Arrange four cutlets in a circle on a large, flat ovenproof plate lined with absorbent kitchen paper and microwave on HIGH for 4 minutes, turning them over halfway during the cooking time. Repeat with the remaining cutlets. Drain on absorbent kitchen paper and serve with baked potatoes and salad.

Serves 4.

SPAGHETTI WITH ANCHOVY AND TOMATO SAUCE

400 g (14 oz) spaghetti
salt and pepper
50 g (2 oz) can anchovies
30 ml (2 tbsp) vegetable oil
1 medium onion, skinned and thinly sliced
397 g (14 oz) can tomatoes with their juice
5 ml (2 level tsp) tomato purée
1 garlic clove, skinned and crushed
30 ml (2 tbsp) chopped fresh parsley
30 ml (2 level tbsp) drained capers
chopped fresh parsley, to garnish

1 Place the pasta in a 2.6 litre (4½ pint) ovenproof glass bowl. Pour over 1.7 litres (3 pints) boiling water and add salt to taste. Cover with cling film and microwave on HIGH for 7 minutes. Leave to stand, covered.

2 Place the oil from the can of anchovies and 15 ml (1 tbsp) of the vegetable oil in a large ovenproof glass bowl. Stir in the onion and microwave on HIGH for 5–7 minutes or until soft.

3 Add the rest of the ingredients except for the remaining vegetable oil and mix thoroughly. Microwave on HIGH for 5–6 minutes, until slightly reduced, stirring occasionally.

4 Drain the pasta, tip it into a heated serving bowl and toss it with the remaining oil. Microwave on HIGH for 1 minute.

5 Pour over the sauce and serve immediately, garnished with chopped parsley.

Serves 4.

TAGLIATELLE WITH CREAM AND MUSHROOM SAUCE

400 g (14 oz) tagliatelle
salt and pepper
25 g (1 oz) butter or margarine
125 g (6 oz) mushrooms, sliced
1 garlic clove, skinned and crushed
30 ml (2 tbsp) dry white wine (optional)
150 ml (½ pint) double cream
30 ml (2 level tbsp) grated Parmesan
30 ml (2 tbsp) chopped fresh parsley

1 Place the pasta in a 2.6 litre (4½ pint) ovenproof glass bowl. Pour over 1.7 litres (3 pints) boiling water, add salt to taste. Cover with cling film and microwave on HIGH for 7 minutes. Leave to stand, covered.

2 Place the butter in a large bowl and microwave on HIGH for 30 seconds or until melted. Add the mushrooms and garlic and microwave on HIGH for 2 minutes.

3 Add the wine and cream and mix thoroughly. Microwave on HIGH for 5–6 minutes or until boiling and slightly reduced, stirring occasionally.

4 Stir in the cheese and parsley and season well with salt and pepper.

5 Drain the pasta and carefully mix with the sauce. Microwave on HIGH for 1 minute. Serve with extra Parmesan cheese.

Serves 4.

BREADS
AND
BAKING

It is possible to bake bread in a microwave oven although you will not get the crisp crust that a conventional oven produces. As white bread tends to look pallid when it is cooked in a microwave, use wholemeal or wheatmeal flour and add ingredients such as sesame seeds or nuts to improve its appearance.

Cakes, too, need some cosmetic treatment if ones such as Victoria sandwich and queen cakes are not to appear white. Use dark coloured ingredients such as chocolate, brown sugars, malt extract, treacle and molasses, and coloured spices such as ginger and cinnamon to improve their appearance. Otherwise, ice or decorate cakes to make them look attractive.

When baking cakes a round container is best and, in particular, a ring mould to ensure even overall cooking. Cakes will cook faster in shallow containers than in deep ones. If you use a loaf tin the cake will tend to cook at the ends before the middle is done. A way to avoid this problem is to cover the ends with smooth pieces of foil once they are almost cooked. Another general point, if you cover cakes with cling film when cooking, it makes them moister.

Cakes tend to look uncooked when they are taken out of the microwave, but the standing time completes the process. Once this is over, immediately turn out the cake to prevent it sticking to the container and peel off any greaseproof paper which may have been used to line it. The top will be very soft so put a tea-towel over the top of the cooling rack to prevent it cutting into the surface of the cake, or invert it. Wait until the cake is cold before icing it. Remember that the middle may still be warm after the sides have cooled.

Crisp biscuits do not cook well in a microwave but the stickier types, such as flapjacks, which are cooked in one piece and then cut into squares or bars, produce good results. Bear in mind that this type of biscuit has a high sugar content which attracts microwaves strongly and it is therefore important to avoid overcooking them.

When preparing containers for either bread, cakes or biscuits grease them lightly and then line them with greaseproof paper. Some plastic containers may need no initial greasing unless the mixture contains only a small amount of fat. Whatever container used, do not flour the inside as this will form a crust on the surface.

DEFROSTING BAKED GOODS AND PASTRY DOUGH

To absorb the moisture of thawing cakes, breads and pastry, place them on absorbent kitchen paper (remove as soon as defrosted to prevent sticking). For greater crispness, place baked goods and the paper on a microwave rack or elevate food on an upturned bowl to allow the air to circulate underneath.

Type	Quantity	Approximate time on LOW setting	Special instructions
BREAD			
Loaf, whole	1 large	6–8 minutes	*Uncover* and place on absorbent kitchen paper.
Loaf, whole	1 small	4–6 minutes	*Turn* over during defrosting.
			Stand for 5–15 minutes.
Loaf, sliced	1 large	6–8 minutes	*Defrost* in original wrapper but remove any
Loaf, sliced	1 small	4–6 minutes	metal tags.
			Stand for 10–15 minutes.
Slice of bread	25 g (1 oz)	10–15 seconds	*Place* on absorbent kitchen paper.
			Time carefully.
			Stand for 1–2 minutes.
Bread rolls, tea-cakes,	2	15–20 seconds	*Place* on absorbent kitchen paper.
scones, etc.	4	25–35 seconds	*Time* carefully.
			Stand for 2–3 minutes.
Crumpets	2	15–20 seconds	As for bread rolls above.
CAKES AND PASTRIES			
Cakes	2 small	30–60 seconds	*Place* on absorbent kitchen paper.
	4 small	1–1½ minutes	*Stand* for 5 minutes.
Sponge cake	450 g (1 lb)	1–1½ minutes	*Place* on absorbent kitchen paper.
			Test and turn after 1 minute.
			Stand for 5 minutes.
Jam doughnuts	2	45–60 seconds	*Place* on absorbent kitchen paper.
	4	45–90 seconds	*Stand* for 5 minutes.
Cream doughnuts	2	45–60 seconds	*Place* on absorbent kitchen paper.
	4	1¼–1¾ minutes	*Check* after half the defrosting time.
			Stand for 10 minutes.
Cream éclairs	2	45 seconds	*Stand* for 5–10 minutes.
	4	1–1½ minutes	*Stand* for 15–20 minutes.
Choux buns	4 small	1–1½ minutes	*Stand* for 20–30 minutes.
PASTRY			
Shortcrust and puff	227 g (8 oz) packet	1 minute	*Stand* for 20 minutes.
	397 g (14 oz) packet	2 minutes	*Stand* for 20–30 minutes.

WHOLEMEAL BREAD

900 ml (1½ pints) tepid water
50 g (2 oz) fresh yeast or 30 ml (2 level tbsp) dried
  yeast and 5 ml (1 tsp) honey
1.4 kg (3 lb) plain wholemeal flour
30 ml (2 level tbsp) demerara sugar
20 ml (4 level tsp) salt
25 g (1 oz) margarine, for greasing
cracked wheat, for sprinkling

1 Put 300 ml (½ pint) of the tepid water in a measuring jug or bowl and stir in the fresh yeast until it is dissolved. Or, if using dried yeast, stir the honey into 300 ml (½ pint) of the water, sprinkle in the yeast and leave it in a warm place for about 15 minutes until it is frothy.

2 Mix the flour, sugar and salt together in a large mixing bowl and make a well in the centre. Pour in the yeast liquid and the remaining water. Mix together to make a firm dough, adding a little more water if necessary.

3 Knead the dough on a very lightly floured work surface and knead it for at least 10 minutes until it is very smooth and elastic and no longer sticky.

4 Place the dough in a bowl, cover it with a clean tea-towel and leave it in a warm place until it has doubled in size – about 1 hour, depending on room temperature.

5 Grease four 450 g (1 lb) ovenproof glass or plastic loaf dishes.

6 Turn the risen dough on to a lightly floured work surface and knead it with clenched fists to 'knock back' the dough, to remove all the large air bubbles. Knead the dough once again for about 5 minutes until it is smooth.

7 Divide the dough into four equal-sized pieces, shape and press these into the prepared dishes, pressing the dough well into the corners.

8 Loosely cover the loaves with a clean tea-towel and leave them in a warm place to double in size and to rise almost to the top of the dishes.

9 Brush the tops of the loaves with a little salted water and sprinkle them with the cracked wheat.

10 Microwave the loaves one at a time on HIGH for 5 minutes. Next, turn out each loaf upside down on to a double thickness of absorbent kitchen paper and microwave on HIGH for 1 minute or until they sound hollow when they are tapped on the base, or until a wooden cocktail stick or skewer inserted in them comes out clean. Cool on a wire rack.

Makes four 450 g (1 lb) loaves.

WHOLEMEAL SESAME ROLLS

1 quantity of wholemeal bread dough (see previous
  recipe)
a little milk, for brushing
sesame seeds

1 Make up the bread dough as instructed in the recipe for Wholemeal Bread, following the directions to the end of step 4.

2 Cut off 50 g (2 oz) pieces of dough and shape them into neat rolls.

3 Place the rolls on large, greased, flat ovenproof plates, 4 to 6 rolls to a plate. Loosely cover the rolls with a clean tea-towel and leave them in a warm place for about 1 hour until they double in size.

4 Brush the rolls with a little milk, then sprinkle them with sesame seeds.

5 Microwave the rolls one plate at a time on HIGH for 3 minutes until they sound hollow when tapped on the base. Cool the rolls on a wire cooling rack.

Makes 36 rolls.

IRISH SODA BREAD

450 g (1 lb) wholemeal flour, plus extra for sifting
5 ml (1 level tsp) salt
5 ml (1 level tsp) bicarbonate of soda
15 g (½ oz) butter or margarine
10 ml (2 level tsp) cream of tartar
5 ml (1 level tsp) Barbados sugar
300 ml (½ pint) milk

1 Lightly grease a large, flat ovenproof plate or microwave baking tray. Mix the flour, salt and bicarbonate of soda in a mixing bowl and rub in the butter until the mixture resembles fine breadcrumbs.

2 Dissolve the cream of tartar and sugar into the milk and use this to bind the flour together, adding a little more milk if necessary.

3 Knead the dough on a lightly floured work surface until it is firm and smooth and there are no cracks.

4 Flatten out the dough to a round about 18 cm (7 inches) in diameter and place it on the prepared plate or tray.

5 Brush the surface of the dough with a little milk and mark a deep cross on the top with a knife. Sift a little flour on top.

6 Microwave on HIGH for 9 minutes, giving the dish a quarter turn three times during the cooking time, until the bread is well risen and dry on top, then turn it over and microwave on HIGH for 1–1½ minutes or until the surface looks cooked. Cool on a wire rack for 5 minutes, then serve warm.

Makes one 450 g (1 lb) loaf.

HERBED CHEESE BREAD

225 g (8 oz) self-raising wholemeal flour
salt and pepper
5 ml (1 level tsp) mustard powder
15 ml (1 tbsp) snipped fresh chives
30 ml (2 tbsp) chopped fresh parsley
150 g (5 oz) Cheddar cheese, grated
25 g (1 oz) butter or margarine
1 egg, size 2, beaten
225 ml (8 fl oz) milk

1 Grease a 1.1 litre (2 pint) ovenproof loaf dish and line the base with greaseproof paper.

2 Mix the flour, salt, pepper, mustard, fresh herbs and 100 g (4 oz) of the cheese together in a mixing bowl.

3 Put the butter into a small ovenproof mixing bowl and microwave on HIGH for 45 seconds until the butter melts.

4 Mix together the butter, the egg and milk, pour this into the flour and mix well to form a soft dropping consistency. Spoon the mixture into the prepared dish, smooth the top and shield the ends of the dish with small pieces of smooth foil, shiny side in.

5 Cover with cling film and microwave on HIGH for 6 minutes until the bread is well risen, remove the cling film and foil, sprinkle with the remaining cheese and microwave on HIGH for 2 minutes or until a wooden cocktail stick or skewer inserted in the centre comes out clean. Give the dish a quarter turn three times during the cooking time.

6 Leave the bread to stand for 10 minutes before turning it out on to a rack to cool.

Makes one 450 g (1 lb) loaf.

Pasta in soured cream sauce – Pasta shapes with mushrooms, olives and tuna in soured cream is a quick and tasty meal to prepare for the family.
Recipe on page 90.

GARLIC BREAD

100 g (4 oz) butter or margarine
1 garlic clove, skinned and crushed
salt and pepper
1 small French loaf, about 43 cm (17 inches) long

1 Put the butter into a small ovenproof glass bowl and microwave on LOW for about 1 minute to soften it. Beat in the crushed garlic and season very well with salt and pepper.

2 Cut the bread into diagonal slices about 2.5 cm (1 inch) thick. Spread the slices with the garlic butter, then sandwich the loaf together again.

3 Divide the loaf into two and wrap each piece in absorbent kitchen paper.

4 Microwave on HIGH for 50–60 seconds until warm. Do not over-heat the bread as it will become tough. Serve immediately.

Serves 6.

Battenburg cake – This cake, a chequer board of chocolate and vanilla, is a treat to serve for afternoon tea.
Recipe on page 99.

CHERRY AND COCONUT CAKE

100 g (4 oz) desiccated coconut
250 g (9 oz) self-raising flour
1.25 ml (¼ level tsp) salt
125 g (4 oz) butter or margarine, cut into pieces
125 g (4 oz) caster sugar
125 g (4 oz) glacé cherries, finely chopped
2 eggs
300 ml (½ pint) milk
25 g (1 oz) shredded coconut

1 Grease a 1.3 litre (2¼ pint) ovenproof glass ring mould or microwave ring mould and sprinkle with 25 g (1 oz) of the desiccated coconut, spreading any excess evenly in the base of the mould.

2 Put the flour and the salt into a mixing bowl and rub in the butter until the mixture resembles fine breadcrumbs. Stir in the desiccated coconut, sugar and cherries.

3 Add the eggs and milk and then beat well, adding more milk, if necessary, to make a soft dropping consistency. Spoon the mixture into the prepared dish, smooth the top and scatter the shredded coconut over the top.

4 Cover loosely with cling film and microwave on HIGH for 10–11 minutes until the cake is well risen and just dry on the surface. A wooden cocktail stick or skewer should come out clean when inserted into the centre. Give the cake a quarter turn four times during the cooking time.

5 Allow the cake to stand in its dish for 10 minutes before carefully turning it out on to a rack to cool.

Serves 8–10.

CHOCOLATE CAKE

175 g (6 oz) butter or margarine
175 g (6 oz) dark brown sugar
3 eggs, beaten
175 g (6 oz) self-raising wholemeal flour
25 g (1 oz) cocoa
60 ml (4 tbsp) milk

For the filling:
75 g (3 oz) butter or margarine
175 g (6 oz) icing sugar
40 g (1½ oz) plain chocolate
15 ml (1 tbsp) milk

1 Grease and line the base of a 20.5 cm (8 inch) round cake dish or soufflé dish.

2 Cream the butter and sugar together until pale and fluffy. Add the eggs a little at a time, beating well after each addition. Add the flour and cocoa and fold in using a metal spoon. Stir in enough milk to give a very soft dropping consistency.

3 Spoon the mixture into the prepared dish and microwave on HIGH for 8–9 minutes or until a wooden cocktail stick inserted in the centre comes out clean. Give the cake a quarter turn three times during cooking. Allow the cake to stand in its dish for 5 minutes, then turn it out and cool it on a wire rack.

4 To make the filling, cream the butter until soft. Gradually sift and beat in the sugar.

5 Break the chocolate into small pieces, place in a small ovenproof glass bowl and microwave on LOW for 2–2½ minutes until melted. Stir into the butter mixture with the milk and beat until smooth.

6 Cut the cake in half and sandwich it together with half of the icing. Swirl the rest of the icing on top of the cake with a palette knife.

Serves 8.

FRUITED BUTTERSCOTCH RING

about 200 ml (7 fl oz) milk
25 g (1 oz) fresh yeast or 15 ml (1 level tbsp) dried yeast and a pinch of sugar
400 g (14 oz) strong plain flour
5 ml (1 level tsp) salt
40 g (1½ oz) butter or margarine
1 egg, size 2, beaten

For the topping:
50 g (2 oz) butter
50 g (2 oz) soft light brown sugar
30 ml (2 tbsp) golden syrup
100 g (4 oz) mixed dried fruit

1 Grease a 2.3 litre (4 pint) ovenproof glass or microwave ring mould.

2 Put the milk in an ovenproof measuring jug and microwave on HIGH for about 1 minute until the milk is tepid. Add the fresh yeast and stir it until it is dissolved. If using dried yeast and sugar, sprinkle it into the milk and leave it in a warm place for 15 minutes until frothy.

3 Sift the flour and the salt into an ovenproof glass bowl and microwave on HIGH for 30 seconds to warm the flour. Rub the butter into the flour.

4 Make a well in the centre of the flour and pour in the yeast liquid and the egg. Mix the ingredients together to form a soft dough.

5 Knead the dough on a lightly floured work surface for 10 minutes until it becomes smooth and elastic. Place the dough in a mixing bowl and cover it with a clean tea-towel. Leave the dough in a warm place for about 1 hour until it has doubled in size.

6 For the topping, put the butter, sugar and syrup into an ovenproof glass bowl and microwave on HIGH for 1–2 minutes, stirring frequently, until melted and boiling. Pour this into the prepared ring mould and then sprinkle it with half the dried fruit.

7 Turn the risen dough on to a lightly floured work surface and knead it again for about 3 minutes until it becomes smooth. Cut the dough into about 24 small even pieces and shape them into balls.

8 Arrange the balls of dough in the ring mould in loose layers, sprinkling them with the remaining dried fruit. Cover the dough loosely with a clean tea-towel and leave it in a warm place until it nearly reaches the top of the mould.

9 Microwave on HIGH for 5–6 minutes until the ring is well risen and cooked and a wooden cocktail stick or skewer inserted in the dough comes out clean. Give the dish a quarter turn three times during the cooking time.

10 Leave the fruited butterscotch ring in the mould for 10 minutes before turning it out on to a rack to cool.

Serves 10.

BATTENBURG CAKE

175 g (6 oz) butter or margarine
175 g (6 oz) caster sugar
few drops of vanilla flavouring
3 eggs, size 2, beaten
175 g (6 oz) self-raising flour
30–60 ml (2–4 tbsp) milk
30 ml (2 level tbsp) cocoa powder
120 ml (8 level tbsp) apricot jam
225 g (8 oz) marzipan
caster sugar, to dredge

1 Grease a shallow ovenproof glass dish about 18 × 23 cm (7 × 9 inches). Line the base with greaseproof paper. Divide the dish in half lengthways with a wall of greaseproof paper.

2 Cream the butter and sugar together until they become pale and fluffy. Beat in the vanilla flavouring. Add the eggs, a little at a time, beating them well between each addition. Carefully fold in the flour. Add 30 ml (2 tbsp) milk to make a soft dropping consistency.

3 Spoon half of the mixture into one side of the prepared dish and smooth the top.

4 Add the cocoa powder, and a little more milk, if necessary, to the remaining mixture. Spoon this into the other side of the prepared dish and smooth the top.

5 Shield each end of the dish with a small piece of smooth foil, shiny side in. Cover with cling film and microwave on HIGH for 7–8 minutes, giving the dish a quarter turn three times during the cooking time.

6 Remove the foil and cling film, allow the sponges to cool in the dish for 4–5 minutes, then carefully turn them out on to a rack to cool.

7 Neatly trim the two sponges to an equal size. Cut each sponge in half lengthways.

8 Put the apricot jam into a small ovenproof glass bowl and microwave on HIGH for 1½–2 minutes, stirring frequently, until hot.

9 Spread one side of one piece of the vanilla sponge with apricot jam and then place one piece of the chocolate sponge next to it and press the two firmly together.

10 Spread more jam on top of the two halves and place the remaining two sponges on top, alternating the colours.

11 Roll out the marzipan to an oblong long enough to go around the sponge cakes.

12 Brush the marzipan with apricot jam and place the sponge cakes in the centre. Bring the marzipan up over the sides to enclose the sponges. Turn the cake over so that the join is underneath.

13 Press the marzipan firmly around the sponges to seal. Trim each end neatly. Use a small knife to decorate the top of the cake with a criss-cross pattern. Pinch the top side edges between thumb and forefinger to give a fluted edge. Dredge the cake with caster sugar and place it on a serving dish.

Serves 10–12.

CARROT CAKE

100 g (4 oz) butter or margarine
100 g (4 oz) dark brown sugar
2 eggs, size 2
grated rind and juice of 1 lemon
5 ml (1 level tsp) ground cinnamon
2.5 ml (½ level tsp) ground nutmeg
2.5 ml (½ level tsp) ground cloves
15 g (½ oz) shredded coconut
100 g (4 oz) carrots, peeled and finely grated
40 g (1½ oz) ground almonds
100 g (4 oz) self-raising wholemeal flour
caster sugar, for sprinkling

1 Grease an 18 cm (7 inch) diameter ovenproof ring mould.

2 Cream the butter and sugar together until they are very soft, pale and fluffy. Beat in the eggs one at a time, beating well between each addition. Beat in the lemon rind and juice, spices, coconut and carrots. Fold in the ground almonds and the wholemeal flour.

3 Spoon the mixture into the prepared mould, smooth the top and sprinkle it with a thin layer of caster sugar.

4 Cover with cling film and microwave on HIGH for 10 minutes. Give the cake a quarter turn four times during the cooking time. When the cake is cooked it will shrink slightly away from the sides of the mould.

5 Remove the cling film and leave the cake to stand for 10–15 minutes before turning it out on to a rack to cool.

Serves 6–8.

ALMOND AND CHERRY CAKE

275 g (10 oz) glacé cherries
65 g (2½ oz) self-raising flour
225 g (8 oz) unsalted butter, softened
225 g (8 oz) caster sugar
6 eggs, beaten
pinch of salt
175 g (6 oz) ground almonds
2.5 ml (½ tsp) almond flavouring
icing sugar, to decorate

1 Grease a 2.3 litre (4 pint) ovenproof glass or microwave ring mould.

2 Dust the cherries lightly with 15 g (½ oz) of the flour and arrange them in the bottom of the dish.

3 Cream the butter and sugar together until they are pale and fluffy. Beat in the eggs, a little at a time, adding a little of the flour if the mixture shows signs of curdling.

4 Sift in the remaining flour with the salt. Add the almonds and almond flavouring and mix the ingredients together well.

5 Carefully spoon the mixture on top of the cherries in the prepared dish and smooth the top.

6 Cover with cling film and microwave on HIGH for 12–13 minutes until the cake is done, when a wooden cocktail stick or skewer inserted in the centre comes out clean. Give the dish a quarter turn three times during cooking.

7 Remove the cling film and leave the cake until it is cold. Loosen around the sides of the cake with a palette knife and carefully turn it out on to a serving plate. Sift icing sugar over the top.

Serves 10–12.

CHOCOLATE, DATE AND NUT LOAF

100 ml (4 fl oz) water
75 g (3 oz) stoned dates, chopped
150 g (5 oz) plain flour
25 g (1 oz) caster sugar
2.5 ml (½ level tsp) salt
2.5 ml (½ level tsp) baking powder
2.5 ml (½ level tsp) bicarbonate of soda
25 g (1 oz) butter or margarine
75 g (3 oz) plain chocolate
1 egg, beaten
75 g (3 oz) walnuts, chopped
50 ml (2 fl oz) milk

1 Grease a 900 g (2 lb) ovenproof glass loaf dish. Place the water and dates in a small ovenproof glass bowl, cover with cling film and microwave on HIGH for 5 minutes. Leave to stand, covered.

2 Meanwhile, sift the flour, sugar, salt, baking powder and bicarbonate of soda into a mixing bowl.

3 Place the butter and chocolate in a small ovenproof glass bowl and microwave on LOW for 3–5 minutes or until melted. Add this to the dry ingredients with the dates, egg, walnuts and enough milk to make a very soft dropping consistency. Spoon the mixture into the prepared dish and smooth the top.

4 Shield each end of the dish with a small piece of smooth foil, shiny side in. Cover with cling film and microwave on HIGH for 8–9 minutes, giving the dish a quarter turn three or four times during cooking. Remove the cling film and foil and microwave on HIGH for 1–1½ minutes or until the cake is cooked, when a wooden cocktail stick or skewer inserted in the centre comes out clean.

5 Allow the cake to stand in the dish for 5–10 minutes before carefully turning it out on to a rack to cool.

Serves 10.

FRUITY TEA-CAKE

75 g (3 oz) currants
75 g (3 oz) glacé cherries, chopped
75 g (3 oz) sultanas
75 g (3 oz) seedless raisins
finely grated rind of ½ a lemon
5 ml (1 level tsp) mixed spice
150 ml (¼ pint) cold tea
75 g (3 oz) butter or margarine
75 g (3 oz) soft dark brown sugar
2 eggs, size 2
175 g (6 oz) plain flour

1 Mix the currants, cherries, sultanas, raisins, lemon rind and mixed spice together in a mixing bowl, add the tea and stir well. Cover the mixture and leave it to stand overnight.

2 Grease a 20.5 cm (8½ inch) soufflé dish and line the base with a round of greaseproof paper.

3 Cream the butter and sugar together until they are pale and fluffy, then beat in the eggs one at a time, beating them well between each addition. Mix in the soaked fruits and any remaining tea and then fold in the flour.

4 Spoon the mixture into the prepared dish and smooth the top. Cover and microwave on HIGH for 10 minutes, then reduce the setting to LOW and microwave for 4 minutes, testing after 4 minutes to see if the cake is cooked – a wooden cocktail stick or skewer inserted in the centre of the cake will come out clean. If the cake isn't ready, microwave further. Give the cake a quarter turn four times during the cooking time.

5 Allow the cake to stand in its dish for 20 minutes before turning it out on to a rack to cool.

Serves 8.

BOSTON BROWNIES

100 g (4 oz) plain chocolate
100 g (4 oz) butter or margarine, cut into small pieces
100 g (4 oz) soft dark brown sugar
100 g (4 oz) self-raising flour
10 ml (2 level tsp) cocoa powder
1.25 ml (¼ level tsp) salt
2 eggs, size 2, beaten
2.5 ml (½ tsp) vanilla flavouring
100 g (4 oz) walnuts, roughly chopped

1 Grease two shallow 12.5 cm (5 inch) × 18 cm (7 inch) glass ovenproof dishes or plastic dishes. Line the base with greaseproof paper.

2 Break the chocolate into small pieces and put them into a large ovenproof glass bowl with the pieces of butter. Microwave on LOW for 3–5 minutes until the chocolate is soft and glossy on top and the butter has melted. Stir well until the mixture is smooth.

3 Stir the sugar into the chocolate mixture. Sift the flour, cocoa and salt into the bowl and add the eggs and vanilla flavouring and beat well to make a smooth batter. Stir in the walnuts.

4 Pour half of the brownie mixture into one of the prepared dishes and shield each end with a small piece of smooth foil, shiny side down. Cover with cling film and microwave on HIGH for 5 minutes until well risen, firm to the touch and slightly moist on the surface. Give the dish a quarter turn three times during the cooking time. Repeat with the remaining mixture.

5 Remove the cling film and foil and allow the mixture to cool in the dish. Cut each cake into about twelve squares before serving.

Makes about 24 squares.

GRANARY TEA-CAKES

100 g (4 oz) butter or margarine, cut into small pieces
250 ml (9 fl oz) milk
750 g (1 lb 10 oz) granary flour
10 ml (2 level tsp) salt
25 g (1 oz) fresh yeast or 15 ml (1 level tsp) dried yeast
  and a pinch of sugar
2 eggs, size 2, beaten
75 g (3 oz) currants
50 g (2 oz) chopped mixed peel
30 ml (2 level tbsp) caster sugar
cracked wheat

1 Put the butter and milk into a small ovenproof bowl and microwave on HIGH for 2–3 minutes until the butter melts. Stir the mixture well and cool it until tepid.

2 Put the flour and salt into an ovenproof glass bowl and microwave on HIGH for 30 seconds to warm the flour.

3 Add the fresh yeast to the tepid milk and butter and stir it until it is dissolved. If using dried yeast and sugar, sprinkle it into the milk and leave it in a warm place for 15 minutes until it becomes frothy. Make a well in the centre of the flour, pour in the yeast mixture and the beaten eggs. Mix the ingredients to form a soft dough.

4 Knead the dough on a lightly floured work surface for 10 minutes until it becomes smooth and elastic. Place the dough in a mixing bowl and cover it with a clean tea-towel. Leave the dough in a warm place for about 1 hour until it doubles in size.

5 Turn the risen dough on to a lightly floured work surface and knead it again for about 3 minutes until it becomes smooth.

6 Divide the dough into 16 equal pieces and shape each one into a flat oval. Arrange these on two greased, large flat ovenproof plates in overlapping rings of eight buns each.

7 Loosely cover the dough rings with a clean tea-towel and leave them in a warm place until they double in size.

8 Mix the caster sugar with 30 ml (2 tbsp) water and microwave on HIGH for 1 minute or until it dissolves. Brush this over the dough rings and then sprinkle the cracked wheat over the top.

9 Microwave, one plate at a time, for 5–6 minutes until the tea-cakes are well risen and cooked, and a wooden cocktail stick or skewer inserted in the centre of the dough comes out clean. Or, when the cooked tea cakes sound hollow when tapped on the base.

10 Allow them to stand for 5 minutes, then move them on to a rack to cool. When cooled slightly, brush with the remaining sugar syrup to glaze.

Makes 16.

JUMBLES

150 g (5 oz) butter or margarine
150 g (5 oz) caster sugar
1 egg, size 2, beaten
300 g (10 oz) self-raising flour
5 ml (1 level tsp) grated lemon rind
50 g (2 oz) ground almonds
20 whole almonds

1 Put the butter into an ovenproof glass bowl and microwave on LOW for about 1 minute to soften it slightly, add the sugar and beat well until the butter becomes soft and fluffy.

2 Beat half of the egg into the creamed mixture, then mix in the flour, lemon rind, almonds and the rest of the egg.

3 Form the mixture into 20 walnut-sized balls and place them on large, greased, flat ovenproof plates, about 4 to a plate, spacing them well apart in a circle. Press out with a fork to a thickness of about 0.5 cm (¼ inch). Place an almond on top of each biscuit.

4 Microwave on HIGH, one plate at a time, for about 2 minutes until the Jumbles are cooked, when a wooden cocktail stick or skewer inserted in the centre comes out clean.

5 Allow the Jumbles to stand for 1 minute, then transfer them to a rack to cool.

Makes 20.

ENGLISH MADELEINES

100 g (4 oz) butter or margarine
100 g (4 oz) caster sugar
2 eggs, size 2, beaten
100 g (4 oz) self-raising flour
75 ml (5 level tbsp) red jam, sieved
50 g (1½ oz) desiccated coconut
4 glacé cherries, halved, and angelica pieces, to decorate

1 Grease 8 paper drinking cups. Line the base of each one with a small round of greaseproof paper.

2 Cream the butter and the sugar together until they are very pale and fluffy. Add the eggs a little at a time, beating well after each addition. Carefully fold in the flour.

3 Divide the mixture evenly among the prepared cups. Place the cups on flat ovenproof plates, 4 to each plate.

4 Cover with cling film and microwave on HIGH, one plate at a time, for 1½–2 minutes until the mixture is cooked but just slightly moist on the surface. Quickly remove the cling film. Stand for 1–2 minutes, then carefully turn the cakes out on to a rack to cool.

5 When the cakes are almost cold, trim the bases, if necessary, so that they stand firmly and are about the same height.

6 Microwave the jam on HIGH for 1–2 minutes until melted and boiling; stir well.

7 Spread the coconut out on a large plate. Spear each cake onto a skewer, brush them with the boiling jam and then roll them in the coconut until they are evenly coated.

8 Top each Madeleine with half a glacé cherry and small pieces of angelica.

Makes 8 Madeleines.

CHOCOLATE NUT BARS

100 g (4 oz) self-raising flour
90 ml (6 level tbsp) rolled oats
100 g (4 oz) soft tub margarine
50 g (2 oz) caster sugar
50 g (2 oz) soft dark brown sugar
1.25 ml (¼ level tsp) salt
2.5 ml (½ tsp) vanilla flavouring
1 egg, size 2
75 g (3 oz) plain chocolate
50 g (2 oz) chopped mixed nuts

1 Grease a 23 × 18 cm (9 × 7 inch) shallow, rectangular ovenproof glass dish.

2 Put the flour in a large bowl and mix in the oats.

3 Beat together the margarine, sugars, salt, vanilla flavouring and egg until they are pale and fluffy. Add the flour and oats and thoroughly mix the ingredients together.

4 Spread the mixture in the prepared dish and smooth the top. Microwave on HIGH for 4–5 minutes until it is cooked, when a wooden cocktail stick or skewer inserted in the centre comes out clean. Give the dish a quarter turn three times during the cooking time.

5 Allow the cake to stand in the dish for 3–5 minutes before turning it out on to a rack to cool.

6 Break the chocolate into pieces and put them in a small ovenproof glass bowl. Microwave on LOW for 3 minutes until the chocolate becomes soft and glossy on top and stir it well until it is smooth.

7 Spread the melted chocolate over the cooled cake and sprinkle it with the nuts. Cut the cake into 16 bars just before the chocolate sets.

Makes 16 bars.

PEANUT BUTTER BISCUITS

60 ml (4 level tbsp) crunchy peanut butter
75 g (3 oz) soft dark brown sugar
50 g (2 oz) butter or margarine
1 egg, size 2
100 g (4 oz) self-raising wholemeal flour

1 Cream the peanut butter, sugar and butter together until they are very soft and fluffy. Beat in the egg and then stir in the flour to make a firm dough.

2 Roll the dough into 16 walnut-sized smooth balls. Place them on large, flat, greased ovenproof plates, about 4 to a plate, spacing them well apart in a circle.

3 Press criss-cross lines on each ball of dough with a fork to flatten slightly.

4 Microwave on HIGH for 2 minutes, one plate at a time. Allow the biscuits to cool slightly on the plates, then remove them to a rack to cool completely.

5 Store in an airtight container.

Makes 16 biscuits.

MUESLI BISCUITS

100 g (4 oz) butter or margarine
50 g (2 oz) demerara sugar
15 ml (1 tbsp) honey
50 g (2 oz) self-raising wholemeal flour
200 g (7 oz) muesli
50 g (2 oz) dried apricots, chopped
1 egg yolk, size 2
icing sugar, for sifting

1 Cream the butter and sugar together until pale and fluffy. Add the honey, flour, muesli, apricots and egg and mix well together to form a firm dough.

2 Roll the dough into 16 smooth balls about the size of walnuts. Place them on large, flat, greased ovenproof plates about 4 to a plate, spacing them well apart in a circle.

3 Microwave on HIGH, one plate at a time, for 2 minutes. Allow the biscuits to cool slightly, then transfer them to a cooling rack to cool completely.

Makes 16 biscuits.

FRUIT AND NUT FLAPJACKS

75 g (3 oz) butter or margarine
75 g (3 oz) demerara sugar
5 ml (1 level tsp) cinnamon
25 g (1 oz) dates, chopped
25 g (1 oz) peanuts, chopped
100 g (4 oz) rolled oats
50 g (2 oz) tenderised dried apricots, finely chopped

1 Grease a shallow ovenproof dish, about 20.5 cm (8 inches) round. Line the base with greaseproof paper.

2 Put the butter into an ovenproof glass bowl and microwave on HIGH for about 15 seconds to soften it. Beat the butter until it becomes pale and fluffy.

3 Mix together the sugar, cinnamon, dates, peanuts and oats and gradually work them into the creamed butter.

4 Press the oat mixture into the prepared dish.

5 Microwave on HIGH for 3–4 minutes, giving the dish a quarter turn three times during the cooking time.

6 Allow the flapjack mixture to cool in the dish until it is just warm to the touch, then cut it into 8–10 wedges and allow them to cool completely.

Makes 8–10.

CHOCOLATE AND NUT BISCUIT CAKE

125 g (4 oz) plain dessert chocolate
15 ml (1 tbsp) golden syrup
125 g (4 oz) butter or margarine, cut into small pieces
30 ml (2 tbsp) double cream
125 g (4 oz) digestive biscuits, roughly broken
25 g (1 oz) sultanas
25 g (1 oz) glacé cherries, chopped
50 g (2 oz) walnuts, roughly chopped

1 Butter an 18 cm (7 inch) flan ring.

2 Break the chocolate into pieces and put them in a large ovenproof glass bowl with the syrup and the butter.

3 Microwave on MEDIUM for 3–4 minutes or until the chocolate has melted, stirring frequently.

4 Add the remaining ingredients and mix thoroughly.

5 Turn the mixture into the prepared flan ring and level the top. Mark lightly into ten wedges, then chill in the refrigerator for 1–2 hours until set.

6 Serve cut into wedges.

Makes 10 wedges.

SAUCES AND PRESERVES

Sauces are made more easily in a microwave than on a hob because there is less risk of lumps forming or of burning occurring. This is because the heat is in the food itself rather than being transmitted through a pan. Many sauces can be made in the sauceboat or container in which they are to be served. If you don't want to use them immediately, cover the surface of the sauce with cling film or greaseproof paper to prevent a skin forming and reheat the sauce when it is required. Stir or whisk sauces regularly to ensure that they cook evenly. You can leave a wooden spoon in the mixture while it is cooking.

Sauces which are thickened with egg need care to prevent them from curdling. Practise cooking them on Low before risking the quicker High setting. When thickening a sauce with cornflour or arrowroot, be sure that the thickener has completely dissolved in the cold water before adding the hot liquid to it. When making a meat sauce, cook the meat first on a roasting rack so that the fat and juices run out before it is added to the other ingredients.

Most sauces can be frozen satisfactorily but ingredients such as cream, yogurt, soured cream or eggs should be omitted and added at the reheating stage, *after* the sauce has been brought just to boiling point. Thereafter do not reboil the sauce.

Preserves and jams should be made in fairly small quantities in containers which are at least two to three times larger than the volume of the preserve being made. A glass ovenproof bowl is ideal as there is no risk of the preserve burning on to the base.

As in conventional preserving, fruits with a high pectin content are the most successful. With lower pectin fruits you need to add lemon juice or commercial pectin. Test that the preserve is set in the usual way.

Once the sugar has dissolved you do not need to boil the preserve for very long to achieve setting point. You can speed things up by first warming the opened bag of sugar on High for 3–4 minutes. To sterilise the jars for potting, fill four of them a quarter full with water and microwave on High until it boils. Each jar will reach boiling point at a different time and should be removed from the oven as soon as this occurs. Preserves which you intend to keep should be covered with traditional jam pot seals but short-life products like Honey Lemon Curd (see page 112) can be covered with freezer-quality cling film and stored in the fridge for 3–4 weeks. (This is a particularly good method of making jam when you have only a small quantity of fruit – perhaps something like Alpine strawberries or peaches.)

Chutneys are less likely to burn than when made in a metal container on a hob because there is no direct contact between the heat source and the base of the container in which the chutney is being cooked. Also, the high acid content cannot react with an ovenproof glass bowl as it does with a pan. Chutneys need to be cooked until they become very thick and they should be stirred frequently during the cooking time. You know they are ready when no free liquid remains and the mixture drops from a spoon like thick sauce. Chutneys should not be bottled with metal lids as the acid in them reacts with the metal. They should be allowed to mature for 2–3 months before eating.

WHITE SAUCE

Serve with fish, poultry, ham, bacon, egg and vegetable dishes.

15 g (½ oz) butter or margarine
15 g (½ oz) flour
300 ml (½ pint) milk
salt

1 Put the butter into a medium ovenproof glass bowl and microwave on HIGH for 30 seconds until the butter melts. Stir in the flour and microwave on HIGH for 30 seconds.

2 Gradually stir the milk into the roux and microwave on HIGH for 45 seconds, then whisk well. Microwave on HIGH for 2–3 minutes until the sauce is boiling and has thickened, whisking every 30 seconds. Season with salt and pepper to taste.

Makes 300 ml (½ pint).

CHEESE SAUCE

Follow the recipe for the White Sauce (see p. 19).

Before seasoning with salt and pepper, stir in 50 g (2 oz) Cheddar cheese, grated, or Lancashire cheese, crumbled, and 2.5 ml (½ level tsp) prepared mustard.
 Stir until the cheese melts, then microwave on HIGH for 30 seconds to heat.

Makes 300 ml (½ pint).

MUSHROOM SAUCE

Serve with fish or vegetables such as broccoli, new potatoes and cabbage wedges.

450 ml (¾ pint) milk
½ small onion, skinned
1 small carrot, peeled and sliced
1 celery stick, washed, trimmed and sliced
1 bay leaf
4 peppercorns
50 g (2 oz) butter or margarine
125 g (4 oz) button mushrooms, wiped and sliced
45 ml (3 level tbsp) flour
salt and pepper
15–30 ml (1–2 tbsp) dry sherry (optional)

1 Put the milk, onion, carrot, celery, bay leaf and peppercorns into a medium ovenproof glass bowl. Microwave on HIGH for 3–4 minutes until the milk comes to the boil.

2 Remove the milk from the oven, cover and leave to infuse for 20–30 minutes, then strain and discard the vegetables.

3 Put the butter into a medium ovenproof glass bowl and microwave on HIGH for 1 minute until the butter melts.

4 Stir the mushrooms into the butter and microwave, uncovered, for 1 minute. Stir in the flour and microwave on HIGH for 1 minute. Gradually stir in the flavoured milk.

5 Three-quarters cover the bowl with cling film and microwave on HIGH for 5 minutes, stirring every 30 seconds until the sauce is boiling and thickened and the mushrooms are tender.

6 Season the sauce well with salt and pepper, and stir in the sherry to taste, if using.

Makes 450 ml (¾ pint).

TUNA FISH SAUCE

1 small onion, skinned and finely chopped
2 garlic cloves, skinned and crushed
60 ml (4 tbsp) olive oil
4 anchovy fillets, finely chopped
226 g (8 oz) can tomatoes
200 g (7 oz) can tuna, drained and flaked
salt and pepper
30 ml (2 tbsp) chopped fresh parsley
cooked pasta, to serve (see page 85)

1 Mix together the onion, garlic and oil in an ovenproof glass bowl. Cover with cling film, pulling back one corner to vent, and microwave on HIGH for 3–4 minutes, stirring occasionally, until the onion softens.

2 Add the anchovy fillets and the tomatoes, with their juice, to the onion, mashing up the tomatoes with the spoon as they are stirred in. Three-quarters cover with cling film and microwave on HIGH for 5 minutes, stirring frequently.

3 Stir the tuna into the sauce and season well with salt and pepper. Microwave on HIGH for 5 minutes, stirring occasionally. Stir in the parsley and serve with hot pasta.

Serves 4 as a first course, 2 as a main course.

BOLOGNESE SAUCE

25 g (1 oz) butter or margarine
45 ml (3 tbsp) vegetable oil
2 rashers streaky bacon, rinded and finely chopped
1 small onion, skinned and finely chopped
1 small carrot, peeled and finely chopped
1 small celery stick, washed, trimmed and finely chopped
1 garlic clove, skinned and crushed
1 bay leaf
15 ml (1 level tbsp) tomato purée
225 g (8 oz) best minced beef
5 ml (1 level tsp) dried mixed herbs or oregano
150 ml (¼ pint) dry red wine
150 ml (¼ pint) beef stock
salt and pepper
cooked pasta, to serve (see page 85)

1 Put the butter and the oil into a large casserole dish, or ovenproof glass bowl and microwave on HIGH for 1 minute. Stir in the bacon, vegetables and garlic and mix well. Cover the dish with a lid or with cling film, pulling back one corner to vent. Microwave on HIGH for 6–8 minutes until the vegetables begin to soften.

2 Add the bay leaf to the vegetables and stir in the tomato purée and minced beef. Microwave on HIGH for 3–4 minutes, stirring two or three times to break up the beef.

3 Add the wine and stock to the dish and stir well to ensure that the meat is free of lumps. Cover with a lid or three-quarters cover with cling film. Microwave on HIGH for 4–5 minutes until boiling, then continue to microwave on HIGH for 12–15 minutes until the sauce is thick, stirring frequently. Season very well with salt and pepper. Serve with hot pasta.

Serves 4 as a main course.

SPINACH SAUCE

50 g (2 oz) butter or margarine
225 g (8 oz) frozen chopped spinach
30 ml (2 tbsp) milk
225 g (8 oz) Ricotta or full fat soft cheese
25 g (1 oz) Parmesan cheese, grated
salt and pepper
grated nutmeg
cooked pasta, to serve (see page 85)

1 Put the butter into a medium ovenproof glass bowl and microwave on HIGH for 1 minute until the butter is melted.

2 Add the frozen spinach to the melted butter and three-quarters cover the bowl with cling film. Microwave on HIGH for 5–6 minutes until the spinach is very hot, breaking up and stirring the spinach two or three times during the cooking time.

3 Stir the milk and the cheeses into the spinach and season well with salt, pepper and freshly grated nutmeg. Reduce the setting and microwave on LOW for 5 minutes, stirring frequently, until the spinach sauce is hot but not boiling. Serve the sauce with hot pasta.

Makes about 600 ml (1 pint).

CUCUMBER SAUCE

A very light sauce to serve with fish.

1 large cucumber
50 g (2 oz) butter or margarine
5 ml (1 level tsp) plain flour
15 ml (1 tbsp) white wine vinegar
150 ml (¼ pint) fish stock or water
10 ml (2 tsp) finely chopped fresh tarragon
salt and pepper

1 Thinly peel the skin from the cucumber, using a potato peeler. Cut the cucumber in half lengthways, scoop out the seeds with a teaspoon and discard them. Finely chop the cucumber.

2 Put the butter into a large ovenproof glass bowl and microwave on HIGH for 1 minute until the butter melts.

3 Stir the sliced cucumber into the butter and three-quarters cover the bowl with cling film. Microwave on HIGH for 6 minutes until the cucumber is very soft, stirring two or three times.

4 Blend the flour with the vinegar and stir in the fish stock or water, then stir this into the cucumber and add the tarragon. Microwave on HIGH for 3–4 minutes until the sauce is boiling, stirring frequently. Season well with salt and pepper.

Makes 300 ml (½ pint).

CRANBERRY SAUCE

Serve with turkey or with cold meats.

225 g (8 oz) fresh cranberries
225 g (8 oz) sugar
150 ml (¼ pint) water
30 ml (2 tbsp) port (optional)

1 Pick over the cranberries and remove any stalks. Rinse the cranberries in a colander under cold running water.

2 Put the cranberries, sugar and water into a large ovenproof glass bowl and mix well. Three-quarters cover the bowl with cling film and microwave on HIGH for 5 minutes, stirring frequently until the cranberries burst and the sugar is completely dissolved. Add the port, if using.

3 Allow to cool completely before serving.

Makes 450 ml (¾ pint).

CELERY BUTTER SAUCE

Serve with carrots, onions and other vegetables such as Jerusalem artichokes.

3 celery sticks, washed, trimmed and very finely
  chopped
450 ml (¾ pint) milk
125 g (4 oz) butter
45 ml (3 level tbsp) flour
salt and pepper

1 Put the celery into an ovenproof glass bowl with the milk. Three-quarters cover the bowl with cling film and microwave on HIGH for 4–5 minutes until the milk is boiling. Reduce the setting and microwave on LOW for 4–5 minutes until the celery is soft.

2 Strain the milk through a fine sieve into another bowl. Reserve the celery.

3 Put 40 g (1½ oz) of the butter into a medium ovenproof glass mixing bowl and microwave on HIGH for 45 seconds until the butter melts. Stir in the flour and microwave on HIGH for 30 seconds. Gradually stir in the strained milk, microwave on HIGH for 45 seconds, then whisk well. Microwave on HIGH for 3–4 minutes until the sauce is boiling and thickened, whisking every 30 seconds.

4 Stir the cooked celery into the sauce and season it well with salt and pepper. Microwave on HIGH for 30 seconds.

5 Cut the remaining butter into small pieces and gradually beat them into the sauce.

Makes 450 ml (¾ pint).

PEANUT SAUCE

Serve the sauce with roast chicken or pork, or with chicken or meat kebabs.

90 ml (6 level tbsp) crunchy peanut butter
75 g (3 oz) creamed coconut, crumbled
300 ml (½ pint) water
20 ml (4 tsp) lemon juice
15 ml (1 tbsp) soft light brown sugar
2.5–5 ml (½–1 level tsp) chilli powder
5 ml (1 level tbsp) tomato purée
1 garlic clove, skinned and crushed
10 ml (1 tsp) soy sauce
salt and pepper

1 Put all the ingredients into a medium ovenproof glass bowl and stir them together well.

2 Three-quarters cover the bowl with cling film and microwave on HIGH for 6–8 minutes until the sauce is boiling and thickened, stirring frequently.

3 Reduce the setting and microwave the sauce on LOW for 5 minutes until the sauce thickens, stirring two or three times during the cooking time. Serve hot.

Makes 450 ml (¾ pint).

SPICY RAISIN SAUCE

75 g (3 oz) stoned raisins
1.25 ml (¼ level tsp) ground cloves
1.25 ml (¼ level tsp) ground cinnamon
good pinch of ground ginger
300 ml (½ pint) water
75 g (3 oz) soft dark brown sugar
10 ml (2 level tsp) cornflour
salt and pepper
25 g (1 oz) butter or margarine
10 ml (2 tsp) lemon juice
cooked bacon joint, to serve (see page 54)

1 Put the raisins, spices, water and sugar into a medium ovenproof glass bowl. Three-quarters cover with cling film and microwave on HIGH for 5 minutes, stirring frequently, until the raisins plump up and the sugar dissolves.

2 Blend the cornflour to a smooth paste with a little cold water and stir this into the raisins. Season the sauce with salt and pepper. Microwave on HIGH for 2–3 minutes until the sauce thickens, stirring twice.

3 Stir the butter and lemon juice into the sauce. Serve with a cooked bacon joint or gammon rashers.

Makes 300 ml (½ pint).

APPLE SAUCE

Serve with pork or sausages.

450 g (1 lb) cooking apples, peeled, quartered, cored and sliced
45 ml (3 tbsp) lemon juice
30 ml (2 level tbsp) caster sugar
25 g (1 oz) butter or margarine

1 Put the apples, lemon juice and caster sugar into a 2.8 litre (5 pint) ovenproof glass bowl. Three-quarters cover with cling film and microwave on HIGH for 5–6 minutes until the apples are soft, stirring frequently.

2 Beat the apples to a pulp with a wooden spoon or with a potato masher. If you prefer a smooth sauce, press the apples through a sieve or purée them in a blender or food processor.

3 Beat the butter into the apple sauce and spoon it into a serving bowl or jug. If the apples are very tart, add a little more sugar to sweeten to taste.

Makes 150 ml (¼ pint).

BARBECUE SAUCE

Serve the sauce with chicken, sausages, hamburgers or chops.

50 g (2 oz) butter or margarine
1 large onion, skinned and finely chopped
1 garlic clove, skinned and crushed
5 ml (1 level tsp) tomato purée
30 ml (2 tbsp) vinegar
30 ml (2 level tbsp) demerara sugar
10 ml (2 level tsp) mustard powder
1.25 ml (¼ level tsp) chilli powder
30 ml (2 tbsp) Worcestershire sauce
150 ml (¼ pint) water

1 Put the butter into a medium ovenproof glass bowl and microwave on HIGH for 1 minute until melted.

2 Stir the onion and garlic into the melted butter, cover the bowl with cling film, pulling back one corner to vent. Microwave on HIGH for 5–6 minutes until the onion softens.

3 Whisk all the remaining ingredients together and stir them into the onion. Microwave uncovered on HIGH for 5 minutes, stirring frequently. Serve hot.

Makes 300 ml (½ pint).

TOMATO KETCHUP

1.8 kg (4 lb) ripe tomatoes, chopped
225 g (8 oz) sugar
pinch of cayenne pepper
2.5 ml (½ level tsp) paprika
15 g (½ oz) salt
75 ml (5 tbsp) white wine vinegar

1 Put the tomatoes into a 2.8 litre (5 pint) ovenproof glass bowl and three-quarters cover the top with cling film. Microwave on HIGH for 40–50 minutes until the tomatoes are very well cooked, very thick and reduced. Stir them frequently during the cooking time.

2 Rub the tomatoes through a nylon sieve into another large, clean ovenproof bowl, then stir in the sugar, spices, salt and vinegar. Three-quarters cover the bowl with cling film and microwave on HIGH for 40–45 minutes until the mixture becomes very thick and creamy, stirring frequently.

3 Pour the tomato ketchup into hot, clean jars. Cover the jars with a clean tea-towel until the ketchup is cold. Cover the jars and store them in the refrigerator for up to 2–3 weeks.

Makes 600 ml (1 pint).

CHOCOLATE FUDGE SAUCE

A luscious sauce for ice cream, profiteroles and other desserts.

75 ml (5 tbsp) single cream
25 g (1 oz) cocoa powder
125 g (4 oz) caster sugar
175 g (6 oz) golden syrup
25 g (1 oz) butter or margarine
pinch of salt
2.5 ml (½ tsp) vanilla flavouring

1 Put all the ingredients except the vanilla flavouring into a medium ovenproof glass bowl and stir them together well.

2 Three-quarters cover with cling film and microwave on HIGH for 5 minutes until the ingredients are boiling hot, stirring frequently.

3 Stir the vanilla flavouring into the sauce and allow it to cool slightly before serving.

Makes 300 ml (½ pint).

EGG CUSTARD SAUCE

Serve the sauce hot or cold with steamed and baked puddings, fruit and mince pies or stewed fruit.

2 eggs, size 2
10 ml (2 level tsp) caster sugar
300 ml (½ pint) milk
5 ml (1 tsp) vanilla flavouring

1 Put the eggs into a mixing bowl with the sugar and lightly beat them together.

2 Put the milk in an ovenproof measuring jug and microwave on HIGH for 2 minutes until the milk becomes lukewarm.

3 Stir the milk into the beaten eggs, then strain this mixture through a nylon sieve into a clean medium ovenproof glass bowl.

4 Microwave the custard mixture on LOW for 6–8 minutes, stirring every minute until the custard thinly coats the back of a wooden spoon. Do not allow the custard to boil as this will make it curdle.

5 Immediately pour the custard into a serving jug and stir in the vanilla flavouring. Serve hot or cold.

Makes 300 ml (½ pint).

HONEY LEMON CURD

finely grated rind of 4 lemons
175 ml (6 fl oz) strained lemon juice
50 g (2 oz) unsalted butter, cut into small cubes
135 ml (9 tsp) thick honey
50 g (2 oz) caster sugar
5 eggs, size 2, beaten

1 Put the lemon rind and juice into a 2.8 litre (5 pint) ovenproof glass bowl. Add the butter, sugar and honey. Strain the eggs through a nylon sieve into the bowl.

2 Microwave on HIGH for 1 minute, then stir very well. Continue to microwave on HIGH for 5–6 minutes until the lemon curd is thick, stirring with a balloon whisk every 30 seconds to prevent curdling.

3 When the lemon curd is thick, remove the bowl from the oven with oven gloves and immediately pour the lemon curd into a cold mixing bowl. Whisk it until it is cool.

4 Pot and cover in the usual way.

5 Store the lemon curd in the refrigerator for up to 2–3 weeks.

Makes about 450 g (1 lb).

Egg custard sauce with apple cake – A tempting dessert which can be prepared and cooked in minutes.
Recipes on page 118 and above.

CRUSHED STRAWBERRY JAM

450 g (1 lb) strawberries, hulled
45 ml (3 tbsp) lemon juice
450 g (1 lb) sugar
knob of butter

1 Wash the fruit, if it is very soiled.

2 Put the strawberries into a 2.8 litre (5 pint) ovenproof glass bowl with the lemon juice. Three-quarters cover the bowl with cling film and microwave on HIGH for 5 minutes until the strawberries are soft, stirring frequently.

3 Lightly crush the strawberries with a potato masher. Add the sugar and stir well. Microwave on LOW for 15 minutes until the sugar is dissolved, stirring frequently.

4 Raise the setting and microwave on HIGH for 20–25 minutes until a setting point is reached (when the skin on a small spoonful of jam allowed to set on a cold saucer wrinkles when it is pushed with the tip of a finger). Stir the butter into the jam.

5 Allow the jam to cool slightly, then pot and cover in the usual way.

Makes 700 g (1½ lb).

MIXED FRUIT CHUTNEY

225 g (8 oz) dried apricots
225 g (8 oz) stoned dates
350 g (12 oz) cooking apples, peeled and cored
1 medium onion, skinned
225 g (8 oz) bananas, peeled and sliced
225 g (8 oz) dark soft brown sugar
grated rind and juice of 1 lemon
5 ml (1 level tsp) ground mixed spice
5 ml (1 level tsp) ground ginger
5 ml (1 level tsp) curry powder
5 ml (1 level tsp) salt
450 ml (¾ pint) cider vinegar

1 Finely chop or mince the apricots, dates, apple and onion, or chop them in a food processor.

2 Put all the ingredients into a 2.8 litre (5 pint) ovenproof glass bowl and mix them together well.

3 Three-quarters cover with cling film and microwave on HIGH for 30–35 minutes until the mixture is thick and all the liquid has been absorbed. Stir frequently during the cooking time, taking particular care to stir more frequently during the last 10 minutes.

4 Pot and cover in the usual way. Store the chutney in a cool, dry, airy cupboard for at least 2 months before using.

Makes 1.4 kg (3 lb).

Fruit kebabs with yogurt and honey dip – A delicious summer dessert which can be made with a wide variety of fruit.
Recipe on page 115.

DESSERTS AND CONFECTIONERY

You can cook all sorts of desserts in a microwave oven – suet and sponge puddings cook in a matter of minutes and you can also make custards, cheesecakes, crumbles and fruit puddings easily. Sponge and suet puddings should be prepared according to the recipe and then covered with cling film which has been pleated to allow for expansion and pricked to allow steam to escape. It is important not to overcook them (the top will cook before the base because of the shape of the basin) and to allow standing time for the heat distribution to equalise.

Fruits with their skins left on should be pierced or scored before microwaving to prevent them from bursting. Fruit with a high water content, such as rhubarb, needs no water added but small berries will need a few tablespoonsful. Dried fruit does not need pre-soaking but should have enough water added to allow it to absorb it to its full size.

Pastry is best cooked in a conventional oven and then reheated with its filling in the microwave. Brush the inside of pastry cases with lightly beaten egg white to prevent the filling from soaking into the pastry.

Pastry and other baked puddings should be reheated on a roasting rack so that air can circulate underneath and prevent their bases from becoming soggy in texture.

Confectionery is quick and easy to make in a microwave and has the advantage that it is unlikely to burn as the mixture is not in direct contact with a heat source. Bear in mind that because confectionery contains a lot of sugar it will attract microwaves strongly and reach a very high temperature. The container – which should be two or three times the size of the volume of the confectionery – will become very hot and you will need to handle it carefully with oven gloves so as not to burn yourself.

Take special care when working with chocolate as it is easy to burn it if you melt it for too long. Use an ovenproof jug if the melted chocolate is to be poured over something and a deep narrow container if you want to dip something like peppermint creams into it. Microwave on Low until the chocolate looks glossy and is soft on top, then remove it from the oven and stir it gently until it is completely melted. If you do overheat it, beat in 2.5 ml (½ tsp) white vegetable fat (*not* butter) and use immediately.

114

DEFROSTING DESSERTS

Type	Approximate time on LOW setting	Special instructions
Cheesecake with fruit topping	about 3–4 minutes for 23 cm (9 inch) diameter cheesecake	*Place* on serving dish. *Stand* for 20 minutes.
Fruit pie	4–5 minutes for 650 g (26 oz) pie	*Stand* for 5–10 minutes. *Do not* make on a metal tin.
Mousse	30 seconds per individual mousse	*Remove* lid before defrosting. *Stand* for 15–20 minutes.
Trifle	45–60 seconds per individual trifle	*Remove* lid before defrosting. *Stand* for 15–20 minutes.

FRUIT KEBABS WITH YOGURT AND HONEY DIP

1 small pineapple
2 large firm peaches
1 large firm banana
2 crisp eating apples
1 small bunch of large black grapes, seeded
finely grated rind and juice of 1 large orange
60 ml (4 tbsp) brandy or orange-flavoured liqueur
50 g (2 oz) unsalted butter
200 ml (7 fl oz) natural yogurt
45 ml (3 tbsp) clear honey
fresh mint sprigs, to decorate

1 Cut the top and bottom off the pineapple. Stand the pineapple upright on a board and, using a very sharp knife, slice downwards in sections to remove the skin and 'eyes'. Cut the pineapple into quarters and remove the core. Cut the flesh into small cubes.

2 Skin and halve the peaches and remove the stones. Cut the flesh into chunks.

3 Peel the bananas and then slice them into thick chunks. Quarter and core the apples but do not skin them. Cut each quarter in half cross-ways.

4 Put all the fruit together in a bowl. Mix the orange rind and juice with the brandy or liqueur, pour this over the fruit and cover and leave to marinate for at least 30 minutes.

5 Thread the fruit on to eight wooden kebab skewers. Put the butter in a small ovenproof bowl and microwave on LOW for 2 minutes, or until melted, then brush this over the kebabs.

6 Arrange the kebabs in a double layer on a roasting rack in a shallow ovenproof dish. Microwave on HIGH for 2 minutes, then re-position the kebabs so that the inside skewers are moved to the outside of the dish. Microwave on HIGH for about 4 minutes, re-position twice more and baste with any juices in the dish. Allow the kebabs to stand for 5 minutes.

7 Whisk together the yogurt and 30 ml (2 level tbsp) of the honey. Pour the mixture into an ovenproof serving bowl, cover with cling film and microwave on HIGH for 1 minute, stirring occasionally, until just warm. Drizzle over the remaining honey and decorate the dip with a few fresh mint sprigs.

8 Serve the fruit kebabs with the yogurt dip handed separately.

Serves 4.

HOT FRUIT SALAD

100 g (4 oz) dried apricots
100 g (4 oz) dried figs
2 large firm bananas, peeled and thickly sliced
2 large fresh peaches, skinned, halved, stoned and sliced
2 large oranges, peel and pith removed, and cut into
  segments
juice of 2 lemons
50 g (2 oz) stoned raisins
5 ml (1 level tsp) ground cinnamon
2.5 ml (½ level tsp) ground ginger
6 cloves

1 Put the dried apricots and figs into a large ovenproof serving dish and add 450 ml (¾ pint) cold water. Three-quarters cover the fruits with cling film and microwave on HIGH for 10–12 minutes, until the fruits are almost tender. Stir two or three times during cooking.

2 Add the remaining fruits, lemon juice, raisins and spices and stir well. Microwave on HIGH for 4–5 minutes until very hot but not boiling.

Serves 4–6.

BAKED APPLES

50 g (2 oz) sultanas
50 g (2 oz) seedless raisins
50 g (2 oz) tenderised dried apricots, chopped
50 g (2 oz) demerara sugar
4 medium cooking apples
60 ml (4 tbsp) water
15 g (½ oz) butter or margarine

1 Mix the sultanas, raisins, chopped apricots and sugar together.

2 Make a shallow cut through the skin around the middle of each apple. Remove the core from each, making a hole large enough to accommodate the filling.

3 Stand the apples in an ovenproof dish and fill the centres with the mixed fruit. Pour the water into the dish and dot each apple with the butter.

4 Loosely cover the apples with cling film and microwave on HIGH for 5–8 minutes, giving the dish a quarter turn three times during the cooking time. Allow the apples to stand for 5 minutes before serving.

Serves 4.

GINGER PEARS

300 ml (½ pint) sweet cider
100 g (4 oz) caster sugar
strip of lemon peel
1.25 ml (¼ level tsp) ground ginger
6 large eating pears, peeled, left whole with stalks on
50 g (2 oz) crystallised or stem ginger, chopped

1 Put the cider, sugar, lemon peel and ginger into a casserole dish. Microwave on HIGH for 3–5 minutes until boiling, stirring frequently to dissolve the sugar.

2 Place the pears in the ginger syrup, spooning it over them to coat. Three-quarters cover the dish with cling film, or with a lid.

3 Microwave the pears on HIGH for 5–7 minutes until they are just tender when pierced with the tip of a knife, turning the pears and re-positioning them in the dish two or three times during the cooking time.

4 Lift the pears from the syrup with a slotted draining spoon and place them in a serving dish.

5 Microwave the syrup, uncovered, for 15–17 minutes on HIGH until the syrup is reduced by half.

6 Pour the syrup over the pears and allow them to cool, then cover and refrigerate the pears until they are well chilled. Sprinkle the chopped ginger over the pears just before serving.

Serves 6.

ORANGES IN CARAMEL

8 medium juicy oranges
225 g (8 oz) caster sugar
200 ml (7 fl oz) boiling water
30 ml (2 tbsp) orange-flavoured liqueur

1 Using a potato peeler, thinly pare the rind from two of the oranges, taking care not to peel off any of the white pith. Cut the rind into very fine julienne strips.

2 Remove the peel and the white pith from all the oranges. Slice the oranges into rounds and remove the pips. In a shallow serving dish, arrange the slices so that they overlap and set aside.

3 Put 90 ml (6 tbsp) water into an ovenproof dish and microwave on HIGH for 1–2 minutes until boiling, then add the sugar and stir until dissolved.

4 Microwave the sugar syrup on HIGH for 5–6 minutes until it turns a golden caramel colour. Immediately pour the boiling water on to the caramel. Add the julienne strips and microwave on HIGH for 4–5 minutes to dissolve the caramel and until the julienne strips are tender.

5 Remove the caramel syrup from the oven and stir in the orange-flavoured liqueur. Allow the syrup to stand for 10 minutes to ensure that all the caramel has dissolved.

6 Pour the caramel syrup and the julienne strips over the sliced oranges. Cover and refrigerate them for about 1 hour until they are well chilled.

Serves 4.

FRUITY SUET PUDDING

175 g (6 oz) cooking apples, peeled, quartered and
*   sliced*
175 g (6 oz) plums, halved, and stones removed
225 g (8 oz) blackberries, hulls removed
finely grated rind of 1 lemon
15 ml (1 tbsp) lemon juice
100–500 g (2–4 oz) caster sugar
175 g (6 oz) self-raising flour
15 ml (1 level tbsp) caster sugar
75 g (3 oz) shredded suet
milk, to mix
custard or ice cream, to serve

1 Grease a 1.4 litre (2½ pint) microwave pudding basin. Line the bottom of the basin with a small round of greaseproof paper.

2 Place the prepared fruits in three separate bowls. Add the lemon rind and juice to the apples with 50 g (2 oz) of the sugar and divide the remaining sugar, if used, equally between the plums and the blackberries. Mix the fruits and the sugar together.

3 To make the suetcrust pastry, put the flour and sugar into a mixing bowl and mix in the shredded suet. Bind the ingredients together with about 60–75 ml (4–5 tbsp) milk to form a soft but not sticky dough.

4 Turn out on to a lightly floured surface and shape into a cylinder, wider at one end than the other. Cut into four pieces.

5 Shape the smallest piece of pastry into a round large enough to fit the bottom of the prepared pudding basin. Place the pastry in the bottom of the basin and spoon in the apple mixture.

6 Shape another piece of pastry into a round large enough to cover the apples. Place on top of the apples and spoon the plums on top. Repeat with another round to cover the plums and spoon in the blackberries.

7 Shape the remaining pastry into a round large enough to cover the blackberries. Cover the blackberries with this final layer of pastry. There should be space above the last layer of pastry to allow for rising.

8 Cover the pudding basin with cling film, pleated in the centre to allow for expansion. Microwave on HIGH for 15–16 minutes, giving the basin a quarter turn three times during cooking. Allow the pudding to stand in the basin for 5 minutes before turning it out carefully on to a hot serving dish. Serve hot with custard or ice cream.

Serves 4–6.

APPLE CAKE

225 g (8 oz) cooking apples, peeled, cored and chopped
100 g (4 oz) sultanas
75 ml (3 fl oz) milk
75 g (3 oz) soft dark brown sugar
175 g (6 oz) self-raising flour
10 ml (2 level tsp) mixed spice
2.5 ml (½ level tsp) ground cinnamon
75 g (3 oz) butter or margarine
1 egg, size 2, beaten
2 apples, quartered and sliced
15 ml (1 level tbsp) apricot jam, heated
custard or cream, to serve

1 Grease a 23 cm (9 inch), 2.3 litre (4 pint) ovenproof glass or microwave ring mould.

2 Mix the apples, sultanas, milk and sugar together.

3 Sift the flour and spices into a mixing bowl and rub in the butter until the mixture resembles fine breadcrumbs. Add the apple mixture and egg and mix the ingredients together well.

4 Spoon the cake mixture into the prepared mould and smooth the top.

5 Cover with cling film and microwave on HIGH for 10 minutes, then remove the cling film and microwave on HIGH for 1–2 minutes until cooked, when a wooden cocktail stick or skewer inserted into the centre of the cake comes out clean.

6 Leave the cake to stand in its mould for 5 minutes before carefully turning it out. Arrange the sliced apple on top of the cake and brush with the apricot jam. Serve the apple cake warm with custard or cream.

Serves 6–8.

CHOCOLATE GATEAU

3 eggs, size 2
125 g (4 oz) caster sugar
30 ml (2 level tbsp) cocoa powder
75 g (3 oz) plain flour
300 ml (½ pint) double cream
822 g (1 lb 12 oz) can apricots, well drained
45 ml (3 tbsp) apricot brandy or kirsch
45 ml (3 level tbsp) apricot jam
chocolate curls, to decorate

1 Grease two deep 15 cm (6 inch) round microwave cake tins or soufflé dishes. Line the bases with greaseproof paper.

2 Using an electric whisk, whisk together the eggs and the sugar until they are very thick and creamy, when they will hold a trail of the mixture for 5 seconds.

3 Sift the cocoa and flour into the whisked eggs and fold them in very carefully.

4 Divide the mixture equally between the prepared dishes and smooth the tops. Microwave, one dish at a time, on HIGH for 2–3 minutes until well risen and firm to the touch. Allow the sponges to stand in their dishes for 2–3 minutes before turning them out on to a rack to cool.

5 Lightly whip the cream. Cut the apricots into slices, reserving a few for decoration.

6 Place one of the chocolate sponge cakes on a serving plate, sprinkle it with half the apricot brandy or kirsch and spread it with two-thirds of the cream. Arrange half of the apricots on top of the cream.

7 Place the remaining chocolate sponge on top of the apricots and sprinkle it with the remaining apricot brandy or kirsch. Spread the remaining cream over the top. Arrange the reserved apricots and the chocolate curls on top of the gâteau to decorate.

8 Put the apricot jam into a small ovenproof glass bowl and microwave on HIGH for 1–2 minutes until the jam is melted and boiling hot, stirring frequently. Brush the boiling jam carefully over the apricots on top of the gâteau.

Serves 6–8.

CHERRY OATMEAL LAYER

25 g (1 oz) chopped hazel nuts
50 g (2 oz) coarse (pin-head) oatmeal
50 g (2 oz) demerara sugar
700 ml (1¼ pints) milk
150 ml (¼ pint) double cream
120 ml (8 level tbsp) black cherry conserve or jam

1 Spread the hazel nuts on an ovenproof plate and microwave on HIGH for 30–45 seconds until they are lightly browned.

2 Place the hazel nuts in a large ovenproof glass bowl with the oatmeal and the sugar, stir in the milk and then refrigerate overnight.

3 Place the bowl of the oatmeal mixture in the microwave oven and microwave on HIGH for 5–6 minutes until boiling, stirring frequently. Continue to microwave on HIGH for 15–20 minutes, stirring frequently, until the oatmeal is tender and the mixture is very thick and creamy. Allow the mixture to cool.

4 Lightly whip the cream and fold it into the oatmeal mixture. Spoon this into four individual serving glasses.

5 Put the black cherry conserve into an ovenproof glass bowl with 15 ml (1 tbsp) water, stir well and microwave on HIGH for 2–3 minutes until the mixture is melted and hot. Spoon this on top of the oatmeal mixture. Chill well before serving.

Serves 4.

CREAMY CHOCOLATE BANANA PIE

225 g (8 oz) plain flour
pinch of salt
50 g (2 oz) butter or margarine
50 g (2 oz) lard

For the filling
100 g (4 oz) caster sugar
50 g (2 oz) plain flour
pinch of salt
450 ml (¾ pint) milk
50 g (3 oz) plain chocolate, grated
3 egg yolks
40 g (1½ oz) butter or margarine
2 large ripe bananas
15 ml (1 level tbsp) soft light brown sugar
30 ml (2 tbsp) lemon juice
225 ml (8 fl oz) double or whipping cream
chocolate curls or grated chocolate, to decorate
  (optional)

1 Place the flour and salt in a bowl. Cut the fats into small pieces and add to the flour. Rub the fat into the flour until the mixture resembles fine breadcrumbs. Add enough water to bind the mixture together.

2 Knead lightly for a few seconds to make a firm smooth dough.

3 Roll out the dough on a lightly floured surface and use it to line a 23 cm (9 inch) flan ring set on a baking sheet. Chill in the refrigerator for 20–30 minutes.

4 Bake blind conventionally at 220°C (400°F) mark 6 for 15 minutes until set. Remove the baking beans and bake for a further 10–12 minutes until golden brown. Remove from the tin and leave on a wire rack until cool.

5 Mix the caster sugar, flour and salt together in a large glass bowl. Gradually stir in the milk, using a balloon whisk and stirring until smooth.

6 Microwave on HIGH for 5–6 minutes until the sauce is boiling, whisking every 30 seconds. Add the grated chocolate and mix well until the chocolate melts and blends into the sauce.

7 Lightly beat the egg yolks with a little of the chocolate sauce, then stir it into the glass bowl containing the rest of the sauce. Microwave on LOW for 5–6 minutes until the sauce is very thick, whisking every 30 seconds, but do not allow it to boil.

8 Beat the butter into the chocolate sauce and immediately pour it into the pastry case. Closely cover the surface of the filling with cling film to prevent a skin forming. Refrigerate for about 4 hours until the filling is set.

9 Peel the bananas and cut them into small pieces, then put them in a mixing bowl with the brown sugar and lemon juice and mash them together well. Spread this over the chocolate mixture in the flan case.

10 Lightly whip the cream, then spread it over the banana mixture so that it covers it completely; mark it into swirls with a palette knife. Decorate the top of the pie with chocolate curls or grated chocolate, if liked.

Serves 8.

VANILLA ICE CREAM

568 ml (1 pint) milk
1 vanilla pod
6 egg yolks, size 2
175 g (6 oz) caster sugar
600 ml (1 pint) double cream

1 Put the milk and the vanilla pod into a large ovenproof measuring jug and microwave on HIGH for 4–5 minutes until the milk comes almost to the boil. Remove it from the oven and allow it to stand for 15 minutes.

2 Put the egg yolks and the caster sugar into a large mixing bowl and beat them together until pale, then stir in the milk. Strain the mixture through a fine sieve into a large ovenproof glass bowl.

3 Microwave the custard on LOW for 20–22 minutes, stirring frequently, until the custard is thick enough to coat the back of a wooden spoon.

4 Pour the custard into a well chilled shallow freezer container and cover the surface closely with cling film to prevent a skin forming. Leave the custard to cool.

5 Freeze the cooled custard for about 2 hours until it becomes mushy, then turn it into a large, chilled basin and mash the custard with a whisk. Lightly whip the cream and fold it into the vanilla custard. Cover and freeze it again for a further 2 hours until it becomes mushy, then mash it again.

6 Cover and return it to the freezer for about 2 hours to become firm. To serve, thaw the ice cream in the microwave on MEDIUM for 30–45 seconds, then leave it to stand for 1 minute until it is slightly softened.

Note: Do not whip the fresh cream if you are using a mechanical churn or ice-cream maker. Agitate the chilled custard and un-whipped cream.

Serves 8–10.

CREME CARAMEL

75 ml (5 level tbsp) caster sugar
450 ml (¾ pint) milk
3 eggs, lightly beaten

1 Place 45 ml (3 level tbsp) of the caster sugar and 45 ml (3 tbsp) water in an ovenproof jug and microwave on HIGH for 5–6 minutes or until the sugar caramelises. Watch it carefully once it starts to colour as it will then brown very quickly.

2 Pour the caramel into the base of a 750 ml (1¼ pint) soufflé dish and leave it to set.

3 Meanwhile, place the milk in an ovenproof measuring jug and microwave on HIGH for 1½ minutes or until warm.

4 Add the beaten eggs and the remaining sugar and carefully strain this over the set caramel.

5 Cover with cling film and place the dish in a larger dish with a capacity of about 1.7 litres (3 pints). Pour in enough boiling water to come half way up the sides of the dish.

6 Microwave on LOW for 25–27 minutes or until the crème caramel is lightly set, giving the dish a quarter turn three times during the cooking time.

7 Leave the caramel to stand for 5 minutes, then remove the dish from the water, uncover the caramel and leave it to cool for about 30 minutes.

8 Refrigerate for about 4–5 hours until the caramel is set, then turn it out on to a serving dish to serve.

Serves 4.

CREAMY RICE PUDDING

225 ml (8 fl oz) full cream evaporated milk
50 g (2 oz) short grain rice
25 g (1 oz) caster sugar

1 Place all the ingredients and 350 ml (12 fl oz) water in a buttered ovenproof glass bowl. Mix well and cover with cling film.

2 Microwave on HIGH for 5–6 minutes or until the liquid is boiling.

3 Reduce the setting to LOW and cook for 35–40 minutes or until the rice starts to thicken. Stir it with a fork every 15 minutes and at the end of the cooking time to break up any lumps.

4 Leave the rice to stand for 5 minutes before serving.

Serves 4.

PEANUT BRITTLE

vegetable oil, for greasing
175 g (6 oz) caster sugar
75 ml (5 tbsp) liquid glucose
1.25 ml (¼ tsp) vanilla flavouring
25 g (1 oz) butter
150 g (5 oz) salted peanuts

1 Lightly oil a large baking sheet.

2 Place the sugar, liquid glucose, 30 ml (2 tbsp) water and the vanilla flavouring in a large ovenproof glass bowl. Microwave on HIGH for 2 minutes, stirring frequently, until the sugar dissolves. Using a wooden spoon, stir in the butter. Microwave on HIGH for 1 minute until the butter melts.

3 Stir in the peanuts and microwave on HIGH for 6 minutes until they are golden brown. Do not stir them during this stage of the cooking.

4 Pour the peanut mixture on to the oiled baking sheet and allow it to cool and set hard. Break it into pieces for eating.

Makes 275 g (10 oz).

CREAMY RAISIN AND CHERRY FUDGE

vegetable oil, for greasing
25 g (1 oz) butter
225 g (8 oz) granulated sugar
75 ml (5 tbsp) condensed milk
2.5 ml (½ tsp) vanilla flavouring
25 g (1 oz) seedless raisins
25 g (1 oz) glacé cherries, chopped

1 Lightly oil a small rectangular foil dish.

2 Put the butter into a 2.8 litre (5 pint) ovenproof glass bowl and microwave on HIGH for 30 seconds, or until the butter is only just melted.

3 Stir in the sugar, milk, 60 ml (4 tbsp) water and the vanilla flavouring and continue stirring for 1 minute until the sugar is almost dissolved. Microwave on HIGH for 2 minutes, then, using oven gloves, give the bowl a gentle shake.

4 Microwave on HIGH for 6 minutes or until a spoonful of the mixture forms a soft ball when dropped into cold water.

5 Carefully remove the bowl from the oven, add the raisins and chopped cherries and beat constantly until the mixture is thick and creamy and tiny crystals form. (Do not continue beating after this or the fudge will become candy-like and granular.)

6 Immediately pour the fudge into the prepared dish. Allow it to cool, then refrigerate it overnight before turning it out and cutting it into squares.

Makes about 350 g (12 oz), or 25 pieces.

LEMON PUDDING

225 g (8 oz) plain flour
10 ml (2 level tsp) baking powder
pinch of salt
275 g (10 oz) soft light brown sugar
175 ml (6 fl oz) milk
30 ml (2 tbsp) vegetable oil
finely grated rind and juice of 1 lemon
2.5 ml (½ tsp) vanilla flavouring

1 Sift the flour, baking powder and salt into a large bowl. Stir in 100 g (4 oz) of the sugar.

2 Make a well in the centre and pour in the milk, oil, grated lemon rind and juice and the vanilla flavouring. Beat to a smooth batter.

3 Pour the mixture into a deep 20.5 cm (8 inch) baking dish. Sprinkle the remaining sugar on top of the batter.

4 Pour over 300 ml (10 fl oz) boiling water. Microwave on HIGH for 12–14 minutes until the top looks dry and the sauce is bubbling through.

5 Leave to stand for 5 minutes. This pudding will separate during cooking to produce a light sponge on top with a lemony sauce underneath.

Serves 4.

RHUBARB CRUMBLE

700 g (1½ lb) rhubarb, washed and trimmed
finely grated rind and juice of 1 small orange
pinch of ground ginger (optional)
75 g (3 oz) demerara sugar
175 g (6 oz) wholemeal flour
100 g (4 oz) butter or margarine
25 g (1 oz) walnuts, finely chopped

1 Cut the rhubarb into 2.5 cm (1 inch) pieces and place in a deep 20.5 cm (8 inch) baking dish.

2 Add the grated orange rind and juice, the ginger, if using, and 25 g (1 oz) of the demerara sugar. Mix thoroughly.

3 Three-quarters cover with cling film and microwave on HIGH for 4–5 minutes or until the rhubarb softens slightly, stirring occasionally.

4 Sift the flour into a mixing bowl and rub in the butter until the mixture resembles fine breadcrumbs. Stir in the remaining sugar and the walnuts.

5 Spoon the crumble mixture on top of the fruit, pressing it down well with the back of a spoon.

6 Microwave on HIGH for 10–12 minutes or until just set, giving the dish a quarter turn three times during cooking.

7 Leave the crumble to stand for 5 minutes, then brown it under a preheated grill if desired. Serve it hot with Custard Sauce (see page 21).

Serves 4.

COFFEE CHEESECAKE

50 g (2 oz) butter or margarine, cut into small pieces
175 g (6 oz) gingernut biscuits, finely crushed
15 ml (1 level tbsp) gelatine
20 ml (4 level tsp) instant coffee granules
45 ml (3 tbsp) coffee-flavoured liqueur
150 g (5 oz) soft light brown sugar
450 g (1 lb) full fat soft cheese
300 ml (½ pint) whipping cream
coffee beans, to decorate

1 Lightly butter a 20.5 cm (8 inch) loose-bottomed deep cake tin or spring-release cake tin.

2 Place the butter in a medium ovenproof bowl and microwave on HIGH for 1 minute or until melted. Stir in the biscuit crumbs and mix together well.

3 Press the crumb mixture firmly into the base of the prepared tin. Leave it in the refrigerator to chill while making the filling.

4 In an ovenproof glass bowl, sprinkle the gelatine on to 45 ml (3 tbsp) water. Leave for 2 minutes to soak, then microwave on HIGH for 30–50 seconds or until dissolved, stirring frequently.

5 Mix the instant coffee, coffee liqueur and sugar with 300 ml (½ pint) water and microwave on HIGH for 1–2 minutes or until the coffee and sugar have dissolved. Stir in the gelatine mixture.

6 Place the coffee and gelatine mixture in a blender or food processor with the cheese and blend until smooth.

7 Lightly whip the cream and fold half of it into the cheese mixture.

8 Pour on top of the biscuit base. Chill in the refrigerator for 3–4 hours until set.

9 Remove from the tin and decorate with the remaining cream and the coffee beans.

Serves 8.

HAZEL NUT TRUFFLES

50 g (2 oz) chopped hazel nuts
125 g (4 oz) plain chocolate
50 g (2 oz) unsalted butter, cut into small pieces
125 g (4 oz) trifle sponge cakes, sieved to make crumbs
50 g (2 oz) icing sugar, plus extra for dusting
15 ml (1 tbsp) brandy
75 g (3 oz) chocolate vermicelli

1 Spread the hazel nuts on an ovenproof plate and microwave on HIGH for 30–45 seconds until they are lightly browned, then cool.

2 Break the chocolate into small pieces and put them into a medium ovenproof glass bowl with the butter pieces. Microwave on LOW for about 1–2 minutes until the butter melts and the chocolate is soft and glossy on top. Remove the chocolate and butter mixture from the oven and stir it well until it becomes smooth.

3 Stir the cake crumbs, icing sugar, hazel nuts and brandy into the chocolate and butter, mixing well.

4 Cover the truffle mixture and refrigerate for about 30 minutes until it is firm enough to handle.

5 Lightly dust your fingers with a little icing sugar, roll the truffle mixture into about 20 small balls and then roll each one in the chocolate vermicelli to coat completely.

6 Place the truffles on a foil-lined baking sheet and refrigerate them until they become firm, then cover them with cling film and keep them refrigerated until they are required.

7 Remove the truffles from the refrigerator 30 minutes before serving and leave them at cool room temperature. Arrange them in a serving dish and serve the truffles with coffee.

Makes about 20 truffles.

QUICK CHOCOLATE FUDGE

100 g (4 oz) plain dessert chocolate
100 g (4 oz) butter or margarine
450 g (1 lb) icing sugar
45 ml (3 tbsp) milk

1 Place the chocolate, butter, icing sugar and milk in a large ovenproof bowl. Microwave on HIGH for 3 minutes or until the chocolate has melted.

2 Beat vigorously with a wooden spoon until smooth.

3 Pour into a 20.5 × 15 cm (8 × 6 inch) rectangular container. Using a sharp knife mark lightly into squares. Leave in the refrigerator for 1–2 hours until set. Serve cut into squares.

Makes 36 squares.

COCONUT ICE

450 g (1 lb) caster sugar
pinch of cream of tartar
60 ml (4 level tbsp) condensed milk
50 g (2 oz) shredded coconut
100 g (4 oz) desiccated coconut

1 Put the sugar, cream of tartar, 45 ml (3 tbsp) water and the condensed milk into a large heatproof bowl. Mix thoroughly.

2 Microwave on HIGH for 3–3½ minutes, or until a spoonful of the syrup forms a soft ball when dropped into cold water. Shake the bowl occasionally but do not stir the mixture or it will crystallise.

3 Stir in the coconut and beat thoroughly until the mixture thickens.

4 Pour the mixture into a 20.5 × 15 cm (8 × 6 inch) rectangular container. Smooth the top and mark lightly into bars using a sharp knife. Leave in the refrigerator for 1–2 hours until set. Serve cut into bars.

Makes 32 bars.

INDEX